YOU

OUGHTA

BE ME

SUSAN MUNROE

HOW TO BE
A LOUNGE SINGER
AND LIVE LIKE
ONE

BY THE FABULOUS BUD E. LUV
AS TOLD TO CORT CASADY AND NED CLAFLIN

ST. MARTIN'S PRESS / NEW YORK

To Alex Bennett
and
Ben Fong-Torres

YOU OUGHTA BE ME. Copyright © 1993 by Robert Vickers. All
rights reserved. Printed in the United States of America. No
part of this book may be used or reproduced in any manner
whatsoever without written permission except in the case of
brief quotations embodied in critical articles or reviews. For
information, address St. Martin's Press, 175 Fifth Avenue, New
York, N.Y. 10010.

Design by Richard Oriolo

Library of Congress Cataloging-in-Publication Data

Luv, Bud E.
    You oughta be me / the fabulous Bud E. Luv.
        p.   cm.
    ISBN 0-312-09947-9
      1. Popular music—Vocational guidance. I. Title.
ML3790.L88 1993
781.42164′023′73—dc20
                                  93-26707
                                      CIP
                                      MN

First Edition: November 1993

10 9 8 7 6 5 4 3 2 1

C O N T E N T S

CONTENTS

CONTENTS

vii

CONTENTS

CONTENTS

ix

AND NOW
A WORD FROM
MR. MILTON BERLE...

Dear Reader:

I remember the night I discovered Bud E. Luv at the Riviera Hotel in Las Vegas. I had just finished my show. I was walking past the kitchen, and there he was—up on one of the steam tables, wearing a little tuxedo, performing for the dishwashers, using a spray nozzle for a microphone. This kid wasn't just wet behind the ears, he was wet *in front* of the ears, too!

He was six years old, and his name was Bud Euripides Luvalopolis Junior. I knew right away his name was too long, his hair was too long, and his pants were too short. But he had talent. He was a great kid, and I made him everything he is today.

So, Bud E., best of luck, good wishes, and, by the way, where's the twenty bucks you owe me?

Love,
"Uncle Miltie"
Beverly Hills, California

Introduction

Of course, you want to be me.

Who wouldn't?

And if you buy this book and read it carefully, you can be something *very close* to me. More than
just a reader. More than just a close personal friend. You
can learn how to be a lounge singer and live like one.

You can practically be a carbon copy of me, Bud E. Luv.

You can possess a jewel-like brilliance all your own and enjoy the very same life-style I do. You can be a swinging cat (or kitten) with all the joys and toys of a lounge legend—limos, jewelry, dazzling clothes, top-notch hair, an adoring public . . . even a legacy.

I'll show you how to have class, style, charisma. I'll teach you what to wear and when to wear it. I'll show you how to let your jewelry speak for you. I'll guide you through the ins and outs of the warm-up suit, the valet, medallions, microphones, medleys, throat lozenges, and more. You'll learn how to walk like a celebrity, act like a celebrity, and schmooze like a celebrity.

Before you know it, you'll look, feel, and smell different. You'll enter a whole new world of culture, confidence, and cologne. Your name will be up in lights, on 8-by-10 glossies, in tabloids, and on talk shows. You'll be living like Dino, Sammy, The Chairman, and The Chief . . . in air-conditioned splendor. You'll have your choice of chicks, 24-hour wedding chapels, bodyguards, ranches, and cosmetic surgeons.

So, say good-bye to the dull, drab, humdrum existence you call your life. Feel the beat! Grab the mike. Get ready for the big note. They're playing *your* song. You're practically me.

Welcome to my Guide to Greatness.

Sincerely,
Bud E. Luv
Las Vegas, Nevada

Talent with a Capital T

Thank you! Thank you very much.
Welcome to my book.
Where're you from?

Great.

Isn't it marvelous what St. Martin's Press has done
with this book?

Feel the pages. The *linen* content is outrageous, isn't it? And what a cover—the weight, the sheen!

Ladies and gentlemen, I love this business we call show. It's my life. And as you know, I've achieved a spectacular number of milestones in a career that has spanned over three decades.

Yes, I've created some musical trends over the years—rock 'n' roll, folk music, disco, bossa nova.

And, of course, I've written hit songs for everyone from Elvis and Frank Sinatra right up to Michael Jackson.

I've been blessed. In fact, I am wearing over thirty-five thousand dollars' worth of clothing and jewelry *at this very moment.*

But what has made it all possible?

Is it luck or fate?

No.

Is it my agent?

No.

Is it *you*, my adoring fans?

Of course. But it's more.

Allow me to share with you the secret that's made this fabulous career such a fabulous reality.

It's a single word that begins with *T*.

The word is Talent.

WHAT THAT CAT UPSTAIRS GAVE ME

When did I know I had it? Immediately. I was born with it. I'll die with it. More than diamonds, Talent is forever.

YOU OUGHTA BE ME

2

But Talent, my friends, must be nurtured. And the real source of inspiration, light, and nourishment in my career has always been my beloved mother, Perithea.

She scrimped, she saved, and never for a second faltered in her faith in my Talent. She pressed my little school pants twice a day, instilling in me the importance of looking immaculate at all times. She bought me imitation gems. I can still remember staring into those gems nestled in my lunch box and seeing my mother's reflection. Later, she taught me how to do my hair. She even bathed me in virgin olive oil on holidays.

By the time I was six, my talent was so obvious that I was discovered by Milton Berle. By the time I was eight, I had made three albums. National tours. TV appearances. The whole enchilada. At the age of nine, I was hanging out with the Rat Pack—Sammy Davis, Jr., Frank Sinatra, Dean Martin, Peter Lawford, and Joey Bishop. I was guiding careers, writing hits, and choreographing shows for too many stars to mention.

Why? Because I had it. I had talent. It wasn't something I had to think about. I didn't have to send away for it. It came to me like jelly on toast. All I had to do was spread it around and give it back, like cream to coffee. (I should mention that I'm enjoying a large breakfast at my ranch as I'm writing this.)

What *is* Talent?

Talent is a playful mistress. A ray of morning sun frolicking on the windowsill. A butterfly. A brooding storm. A way to make a buck.

You can't buy it. You can't fake it. You either have Talent—or you pretend to have it.

YESTERDAY: *FROM LEFT TO RIGHT*, MIKEY LUV, BUD E. LUV, AND MARKEY LUV AT SONIA AND HARVEY'S FAMED CATACOMBS RESORT IN THE CATSKILLS, 1961.

SUSAN MUNROE

SUSAN MUNRO

THE LOOK OF LUV: BACKSTAGE AT THE SANDS IN VEGAS IN '92, RE-CREATING OUR ORIGINAL PUBLICITY SHOT.

Who's Got It, Who Doesn't

How can you spot those who have the Big *T*?

Look for the earmarks. There are telltale signs.

For example, there are very few people in this business we know and love called show who can work with *one* name. We know who they are. Elvis. Cher. Catinflas. Lassie. And a close personal friend—Charo. She has it.

Look in the tabloids. The tabloids always pick on the very gifted.

Follow the bankruptcies. The truly Talented are often preyed upon by armies of hangers-on who bleed them dry and leave them penniless in a ditch.

Who's singing the National Anthem at the Super Bowl? You can bet it's a Super Talent.

And believe me, pal, whoever the comics are imitating the most are the cats and kittens who have the most—Talent, that is.

Look for the relaxed smile, the easy manner with the public. Look at the jewelry—not overstated, but always apparent.

Who has Talent? Many do. Mozart. Da Vinci. Henry Ford. Let's take a closer look.

EYDIE GORME: Elegant simplicity, a capital *T*.

STEVE LAWRENCE: Excess baggage. She's carrying him.

BOBBY DARIN: A genius. The good die young.

DON HO: Tiny bubbles, tiny talent.

MICHAEL JACKSON: A mega-talent. The vitiligo thing was my idea.

TALENT WITH A CAPITAL T

TOM JONES AND A FEW OF MY FAVORITE BABES
CUT ME A PIECE. IT WAS MY BIRTHDAY, BUT
THE BAKER PUT TOM'S NAME ON THE CAKE BY
MISTAKE. *LEFT TO RIGHT:* JOAN RIVERS, JOEY
HEATHERTON, SONNY BONO, TOM, DIONNE
WARWICK, DEBBIE REYNOLDS, AND LIBERACE.

STEVE ALLEN: The schtick—great. The music—this could be the start of something boring. Just kidding, Steverino! See you at my golf classic.

WAYNE NEWTON: Bankrupt or not, always going for broke. A Geronimo with pipes.

WILLIE TYLER AND LESTER: These guys kill me.

NANCY SINATRA: Great boots.

ENGELBERT HUMPERDINCK: Making this name a household word was no easy task. Capital *T*.

FRANKIE AVALON: No.

PHYLLIS DILLER: I love what she's trying to do.

NEIL SEDAKA: Great writer. Sings higher than Wayne, God bless him.

PETER, PAUL AND MARY: Very sincere. Love her, but *two* bald guys on the same stage? It must be 500 miles to the nearest toupee shop.

TRINI LOPEZ: If I had a hammer, I'd hit this clown on the head. But I kid Trini.

DON RICKLES: Yes. Misunderstood, and a close personal friend.

JOHN DAVIDSON: Hair, A-plus.

DONNY AND MARIE: Teeth for days, talent to spare. I loved what they did with my barbershop quartet idea.

TONY ORLANDO: Without Dawn, we're all in the dark.

TOM JONES: Big *T* squared. Almost as good as me. One of my model students.

PAUL ANKA: Undeniable.

PAT BOONE: Nothing but white and green bucks.

ROBERT GOULET: On a clear day, you can see his house from my ranch.

TALENT WITH A CAPITAL T

PIA ZADORA: Career—bought and paid for. I hope she has a receipt.

ASHFORD AND SIMPSON: Too much hair.

SANDLER AND YOUNG: Too much talent.

AXL ROSE: Misunderstood. A sensitive talent.

JUDY COLLINS: Pitch, Judy, pitch. Pick a key and stick with it.

NEIL DIAMOND: I love the moody thing he does.

MADONNA: Definitely has it. She defined *lounge* in the eighties.

DINO, FRANK, SAMMY, JACK JONES, LIZA, MEL TORME, AND TONY BENNETT: What do you think? *T-T-T-T-T-T-T*. Forever.

WHY BILL MURRAY'S A BUM

Las Vegas is built on two things—lounge singing and comedy. Bread and butter. Earth and water. Without music, the laughter is hollow. Without laughter, the music means nothing. Comedy and music need each other.

Bill Murray—comedian—denigrated and disgraced the profession of lounge singing with a tawdry, insincere, and off-key imitation of the work of his brothers and sisters in music. This kind of betrayal is the hallmark of a hooligan, a ragamuffin, and, the worst insult I know, a non-professional.

How would Bill's mother, Mrs. Murray, feel if I, Bud E. Luv, got up and told Bill Murray's jokes without an ounce of feeling or an iota of timing? Bill Murray is an ill-shaved, misshapen bum. May all his sequels be turkeys and all his Christmas releases be bombs.

Actually, I kid Bill. We're very close.

MICHAEL OCHS ARCHIVES/VENICE, CA

THE HATS AND HAT NOTS: *LEFT TO RIGHT,*
DEAN MARTIN, FRANK SINATRA, AND
SAMMY DAVIS, JR.

IF YOU'VE GOT IT, FLAUNT IT!

Does Dolly Parton wear a topcoat? Does Tony Bennett shy away from the Big Finish? Does Tom Jones wear baggy pants?

No. They play (and wear) their strongest suit. They amplify. They *enhance*.

The Chairman phrases. Dino sips. Cher tattoos it. The Chief slam-dunks. Every great lounge entertainer understands the First Commandment of Show Business—Thou Shalt *Maximize*.

Every night when I go onstage, do I blink and hide in the glare of the lights, skulk, whimper a lyric or two, and scuttle offstage? Of course not. I put on a dazzling display of pyrotechnic talent, a musical explosion that makes the cats' jaws drop and leaves the broads drooling in their drinks.

When you've got what That Cat Upstairs gave me, you don't hide it behind the slots. You flaunt it. All the way. You should do the same.

Everyone's got a special talent. Figure out what yours is and practice flaunting it. Try to get applause for what you do well. If you park cars, try parking them at breakneck speed. Park two at a time. If you have a knack for delivering packages, go the extra mile—deliver more. Balance them. Stack the breakable ones sky-high, and then dump them with a flourish and a "who loves ya" wink. Whatever you do, *flaunt* and *maximize* until your customers are on their feet screaming for more.

My Talent:
The Incredible Burden

It's true. Having Talent is a burden. And sometimes the weight is overwhelming.

People often ask me, "Bud E., how do you carry the heavy burden of your talent so gracefully?"

Simple.

I wear a Talent Brace.

Send $49.95 to: Talent Brace, House of Luv, Box 711, Las Vegas, Nevada 85103. No checks, please.

But even so, when you're the special me that I am, sometimes the ordinary Bud E. gets lost. I get confused. The voices blur in my head: "You're the greatest." "You're a legend." "The white zone is for loading and unloading only."

At times like these, I have to catch myself.

What do I do?

I stop and smell the cactus. I go to the desert. I get out of the limo, get away from the marquee with my name on it (in HUGE letters), away from the standing ovations, away from the groupies and *listen.* You should do this, too.

If you can't go to the desert, go into your closet. Close the door. Stand among your clothes in the dark, and listen.

If you've got an enormously large talent like I do, you've got to learn to live with it. Buy a king-size bed for your talent. Remember, you've got to sleep with yourself at night. Add a wing to your house. Your talent needs room to breathe. Wear pantaloons.

Remember, only you can face yourself in that morning mirror framed with all those little light bulbs. No one can do it for you.

When you're feeling the burden, when you're at that painful crossroads . . . stop. Breathe. Wait. Listen.

Touch your medallion.

And remember: Bud E. goes through this every day.

LOOKING TALENTED: TEN THINGS YOU CAN DO

You may be Pavarotti. You may be Caruso. You may be Florence Nightingale or Florence Henderson. You may have all the God-given Talent in the world. But you're not going anywhere if you don't *look* talented. And if you *don't* have any talent, you'd really better *look* like you do.

People often say to me, "Bud E., why do you *look* so talented?"

My friends, I'll tell you. There are secrets. And I'm going to give you ten very basic pointers to help you look as talented as you may or may not be.

1. LOOK UP. Look like you have vision. Talented people don't walk around staring at the ground. Get your chin up! Focus on the horizon.

2. PRACTICE SQUINTING. The very Talented often tighten their eyelids, as if peering dimly into the future. This can work for you.

3. CARRY A PAIR OF GLASSES. Glasses lend an air of intelligence. Put them on occasionally during

LOOKING TALENTED: NOTE THE PAINED, FAR-AWAY EXPRESSION—VERY TALENTED. MY CLOSE FRIEND FIDEL SENT ME THE CIGAR.

conversation, even if there's nothing to read. But don't wear them all the time—you'll look like some two-bit scientist.

4. NEVER CARRY PENCILS OR NOTEBOOKS. These things are for secretaries. Talented people seem to be able to keep things in their heads. And if they forget, it means they're really talented.

5. WEAR LEISURE APPAREL. Look like you have lots of free time, as if you've just come from the beach, the golf course or the tennis court. Talented people don't have to work as hard as normal schmucks.

6. SPEAK SOFTLY. You should act like you're used to being listened to.

7. APPEAR SENSITIVE. Stare at plants. Notice colors, tints, hues. Appreciate fabrics. Everyone knows Talented people can find inspiration in anything. Act like you can, too.

8. IN CONVERSATION, SAY "WAIT A MINUTE!" BE QUIET FOR FIFTEEN SECONDS. THEN, SAY "GO AHEAD." This gives the impression you've just had a brilliant thought you've decided not to share.

9. FORGET TO EAT.

10. CONSIDER WEARING AN EARRING. Not right for everyone, but it can lend a dash of flamboyance. Don't wear it all the time, and *never* wear two.

T W O

A Little Thing Called Style

Style starts with an inner voice. A tiny atom of confidence. A nucleus of faith deep within. And slowly it grows. It grows like a bank account. Outward. Upward. Compounding. Soon you feel it everywhere: in your hands, your eyes, your smile, your *shoulders*. They're broader somehow. Your shoulderpads rest more easily.

This inner sense of Style, slowly emerging, tells your body what to do, what to *wear*, what to *sing* and when. It makes the choices for you, in brilliant colors.

Soon you feel the transformation. The microphone feels more comfortable in your hands. The high notes are easier. Your pants fit better in the seat.

Can it be happening to you? Yes!

I think of style as a coming of age, a rite of passage, an entertainer's puberty. Until you possess a fully developed sense of style you will languish with the Holiday Inn riffraff, slumped over a cheesy synthesizer and a glass of cold house burgundy. If you find a cigarette butt in it, don't be surprised. Until you have style, panache, savoir faire, vichyssoise, chateaubriand, you're not ready for the lounge.

Have It?
I Invented It!

Drench yourself in Style, like I do.

Buy yourself a brilliant canary-yellow wool gabardine suit embroidered with covered wagons and cactus, designed personally by Nudie.

Or slip into an elegant scarlet tuxedo jacket with lucky dice, martini glasses, and playing cards tumbling down the back and sleeves.

Purchase an 18-karat white gold pinkie ring with your name spelled out in sparkling diamonds, your middle initial in sapphire.

You're starting to *feel* the style, aren't you?

Of course you are.

Now spray that lofty mane of blue-black hair until its sheen resembles nothing so much as the luster of a sinewy black panther.

Pick up your platinum cigarette case embossed with an emerald portrait of Sammy Davis, Jr., his good eye a rare Burmese opal.

Move with the sure stride, the easy demeanor, the devil-may-care *Ka-chow, chow, chow* attitude.

Who are you?

That's right.

You're someone with Style.

What makes you sparkle? What makes you special? What makes you expensive?

Style, my friend.

CHARISMA: IT'S EASY

Camelot. Those heady days. Being with Bobby and Jack Kennedy in the Oval Office, entertaining at the White House. It's still a dream, those times in the early sixties. Those nutty Thousand Days.

I remember being with the Kennedy family in Hyannis Port one weekend. Bobby had flown me in from the Catskills with Pat Cooper for a small surprise birthday party for Ethel. There were broads everywhere. I was in the living room when Jack came in from the beach. He'd just been out for a swim. Suddenly, the room stopped. What was it? Was it the towel with the Presidential seal on it? Was it the tousled hair? Was it the swim trunks with the Presidential seal on them?

No.

IN A PUBLICITY SHOT, TEETH SPELL CHARISMA WITH A CAPITAL C. THE OUTSTRETCHED ARMS SAY "COME AND GET ME."

SUSAN MUNROE

It was charisma.

I learned something very special from the president that day—a lesson about magnetism. I learned where charisma comes from. It was more than the compelling vision of this young leader of the free world. It was more than the razor wit, the flashing eyes. It was more than the broads.

The charisma was in his teeth.

When Jack smiled, and I saw him smile many times that day, every atom in the air stood crisply at attention. The glow of his smile warmed the room. It was unforgettable. And I've often noticed that the most charismatic people have . . . The Teeth.

Bobby had an even bigger set. Look at Ray Charles. Sure, there's the music thing, but he had no charisma until he started smiling. The Osmonds. They'd still be steaming towels in a barbershop in Utah if it weren't for their teeth.

Remember, when the Kennedys smiled, the whole world smiled with them. Camelot started with clean enamel. When Carol Channing smiled, you couldn't get *Hello, Dolly* off Broadway with a crowbar.

To get charisma, see your dentist. He (or she) can help. The American Dental Association wouldn't be where it is today if it weren't for the marriage of teeth and charisma. It's a wedding you can't afford to miss.

WHERE TO HANG OUT

If you're going to be a lounge singer, it's important that you hang out in the right places. Don't let where you hang out hang you. Your image is very important. When you're not performing, it's location, location, location.

Here are a few do's and don'ts:

THE LOBBY OF A LUXURY HOTEL. Fine. But always be seen crossing the lobby at a brisk pace. If you have nowhere else to go, it's okay to cross the lobby several times. But always at a brisk pace. Never loiter.

ANY FIRST-RATE COUNTRY CLUB OR GOLF COURSE. Excellent. On the tee, on the court, or preferably in the clubhouse. Here it's important to be seated, relaxing with a group of cronies. (If you don't have cronies, ask the bartender to get you some.)

THE FRIAR'S CLUB ON EITHER COAST. Ideal.

AIRPORTS, TRAIN STATIONS, DOCKS, AND OTHER DEPOTS. Wrong. A lounge singer travels from point to point as quickly, conveniently, and luxuriously as possible. Whenever we can, we bypass the traveling public. Travel is a private matter. Never be seen traveling with the rabble.

RANCHES. Always a good hangout. Makes for great photo opportunities against a fence with mountains in the background. Remember to squint.

FINE RESTAURANTS. Yes. But only between

three and six in the afternoon. And always order breakfast. Ordering any other meal makes you look like you're not working.

THE RACETRACK. Fine, so long as it's top-flight. Hollywood Park, Santa Anita, Del Mar. Get a private box, and never bet. That you do on the phone with your bookie.

OLD, ESTABLISHED RESORTS AND HEALTH SPAS. Perfect. Any of your springs and baths. Stay away from the new trendy spots. You'll wind up in a picture with Stallone or one of those Trump broads and look like a crasher.

BARS AND LOUNGES. Yes, of course. But only where you're working. If you hang out in bars and lounges where you're *not* working, you'll look like an alkie or a desperate swinger.

Okay, you've picked your hangout. You're there. You're thinking: "I've got it covered." But suddenly you're sweating like a pig at auction. You look down. Your wardrobe is clashing with the fabric on the sofa, a magenta nightmare. You look in the mirror and see your face lit up like a French fry under a cafeteria heat lamp. And most important, no one knows you're there. You're on fire, but you're invisible.

What went wrong?

Seating and *lighting*, my friend.

Don't neglect these all-important basics.

Picasso didn't paint a daisy in a Dr. Pepper bottle. He placed the bloom in a tasteful, complementary vase.

When you're hanging out, always place yourself in a premium seat under carefully selected lighting.

You should appear to be glowing from within, not baking like a clam. Oranges and reds are inflammatory. Avoid them. Stay with rose or soft pink. Blue is nice, especially for a cat in a trench coat on a lonely Paris boulevard at night. Use the lighting to accent your off-stage persona.

But people say to me, "Bud E., how do I get the premium seat if someone's already in it?"

Simple. Always carry several crisp fifty-dollar bills wherever you go. Give one to the maitre d' or top-ranking employee in the room, and insist that he show you to the best seat. If another patron's already in that seat, have the maitre d' summon him to an emergency phone call, and then sit down in the seat yourself. When the patron returns and wants his seat back, give *him* a fifty and tell him to take a walk. You'll be surprised how often this works in this economy.

PRACTICING THE CELEBRITY WALK

When a lounge singer enters a room, no one has to ask, "Who is it?" Even if you don't know his or her name, you know by the walk that it's *somebody*.

Lounge singers don't just walk. We saunter. We float. We glide, basking in the applause, real or imaginary. We arrive like a vision; we leave like a dream. Just by the way we move, we leave an indelible impression in the minds of those who have been fortunate enough to see us.

I can't tell you how many times I've overheard people say, "I don't know, there's just something in the way he moves."

Here's why. There are three basic walks you must develop:

THE ENTRANCE GAIT

1. THE ENTRANCE GAIT. Smooth, crisp, purposeful. A graceful stride designed to cover ground. The steps are long, the eyes are straight ahead, we're smiling. Also appropriate for exits. When I first worked with Andy Williams, he needed help getting onstage. He looked like Howdy Doody. His walk was a herky-jerky mishmash of motions. I gave him the Entrance Gait, and he soared with it. Now, Andy comes onstage smiling, confident, a clear winner.

The Entrance Gait can also be used offstage

very effectively. Sammy and I used to call it the
Steakhouse Strut. It's ideal for parties, restaurants,
openings. Basically, the Strut is the same as the
Entrance Gait except, under certain circumstances,
one hand is carried in a trouser pocket. Remember,
no abrupt head motions. Walk like you're the top
attraction. A lounge singer is always the most important person in the room. Sudden movements of
the neck and head imply uncertainty.

25

2. THE LATERAL GLIDE. Easy, effortless, cool. Perfect when you're starting a song. One foot gently takes the place of the other. The upper body is quiet, very poised, almost as if it were moving on a conveyor belt. Great for traveling across the stage.

THE LATERAL GLIDE

3. THE TV TROT.

Light, athletic,
jaunty. The TV
trot subtly suggests the link between sports and entertainment. Designed to show youth and vigor, this step is used by lounge singers to move quickly to new stage positions, especially on television, and dispel any hints of femininity. The TV Trot should never result in sweating or wheezing. Save that for your workout. And ladies, don't do this in a low-cut evening gown.

THE TV TROT

To practice these walks at home, here are a few suggestions: Remove your shoes. Stand on a carpeted floor. (High-low, shag, or sculptured is fine.) Take small, silent steps. A celebrity walk must be noiseless. No army boots on a plank floor! We want feline grace, balance, and timing. The shoulders are high, proud, yet relaxed. The hands are poised at the sides, ready to swing lightly. Remember, the steps are almost minute.

Ready? Begin.

One, two, three, four, five, six . . . AND one, two, three, four, five, six.

Relax the shoulders.

Chin high. Eyes straight, gleaming.

Don't let the hands swing too far. You shouldn't see your nails.

One, two, three, four, five, six . . .

Very good. Feel the crowd buzzing? You're getting more famous with every step.

One final tip: Never walk with food in your pockets. Once, I saw Elvis working at the Las Vegas Hilton with a piece of Black Forest cake in his pocket. The audience couldn't take their eyes off it, bulging under the cape. I doubt that anyone remembers what he sang that night. Even the King couldn't compete with the fudge.

Don't be a lunch wagon. You're a celebrity. Walk like one.

THE WARM-UP SUIT:
WHEN TO TAKE IT OFF

The lounge singer is a lithe, limber creature whose muscles are sensitive yet powerful. Like the pole vaulter, he must be ready to ask his body to perform to the utmost at a moment's notice. The lounge singer lives in a near-constant state of readiness. And yet, when he isn't performing, he requires a garment that provides comfort and style, while accommodating the Spartan discipline that his profession demands.

Sounds impossible, right?

No, my friends. There is an ideal vessel to contain this finely tuned machine we refer to as the lounge singer. This vessel is the warm-up suit.

Appearing first in the early seventies and regrettably made of synthetic fabrics, the warm-up suit was popularized by athletes and television personalities. The warm-up suit quickly became the offstage uniform of the lounge entertainer. From there, it spread to malls, mini-malls, and convenience stores the world over to become one of the most popular garments ever devised by man.

Today, the smart entertainer's warm-up suit is 100 percent cotton—never a synthetic—allowing his refined musculature to breathe. Before, after, and in between shows, the warm-up suit is simply the last word in function and fashion.

Still, as the day follows the night, so must a performer's stage apparel follow the warm-up suit. The question is *when*?

When comes the dawn?

When should you take the warm-up suit off?

The answer is clear: The warm-up suit is an inter-mezzo—no more. It is to be worn in the limousine between the house, the ranch, or hotel suite and the dressing room. It is taken off just before showtime, when you are ready to put on your stage clothes. It may be worn between shows, while your stage clothes are being pressed or allowed to dry and you are greeting the public. It then may be worn *après* show for the limo ride home. At no other time is it to be worn!

If you are wearing your warm-up suit more than four hours per day, you are abusing the garment.

Do not, I repeat, *do not* wear your warm-up suit to meals, friends' homes, charity appearances, while shopping, or while working out.

The warm-up suit is *not* appropriate everyday attire for a celebrity. Do you want to join the faceless army of cigar-chomping agents, hangers-on, personal trainers, and mini-mall employees who live in their warm-up suits? Of course you don't.

PAY TOP DOLLAR FOR EVERYTHING!

Some people say the United States Senate is the most exclusive "club" in the world. Baloney. The Fraternity of Lounge Singers is. And you don't join this fraternity without paying top dollar.

The lounge is no place for whiners. I don't want to hear, "But I was trying to get a deal." "My friend got it wholesale." "It was such a bargain." Hey! Get off my cloud! Does Frank get it wholesale? No. Does Dino

I CALL THIS MY FLORAL JUBILEE. IT'S ANOTHER
NUDIE CLASSIC. THE BOOTS ARE UNBORN
LIZARD CHEEK.

SUSAN MUNROE

scrounge around thrift shops looking for a lambswool V-neck? No, he pays retail at Carroll & Company on Rodeo Drive. And he comes home with a garment he can be proud of. If you have friends who run around paying wholesale, get new friends.

If you're going to be in *this* Club, you must pay and *be seen paying* top dollar for everything you need or don't need. The words *I don't care what it costs, I've gotta have it!* should come as easily to you as breathing.

Believe me, there's no better feeling than walking into a fine haberdashery or an exquisite jewelry store and paying the full ticket price. No one does it. That's why *you* should. It sets you apart. You're above the fray. You look better than the rest. You own the shop. You honor the profession.

Look at it this way. If you pay $5,000 for a suit, you know you're wearing a beautiful hand-constructed $5,000 suit. No one can take that away from you. On the other hand, if you pay $500 for the same suit, what are you *saying*? Are you saying, "I don't have $5,000"? Is that the message you want to send to yourself and others? Are you saying, "I'm only willing to spend $500 on my suit, and I'm putting the other $4,500 into something else"? What? Are you nuts? This is *show business*. This is your *wardrobe*. What else are you putting your money into? Your children's education? Wake up!

Did Liberace pinch pennies so he could beef up his stamp collection? No! He became a legend by wearing every dime of his disposable income. He had Style. And that Style cascaded off his shoulders, dripped from his fingers, and spilled over onto the piano. He made millions paying top dollar. Liberace was a charter member of the

Fraternity of Lounge Singers. I miss him very much.

I want you to join this Club. The Club needs new blood. I wouldn't be writing this book if I didn't want you to have the privilege of being a member. But if you think the doors swing open for bargain hounds, guess again. Quality is never cheap. Style—true style—costs money. Spend it.

AUTOGRAPHS: THE BIGGER, THE BETTER

Nothing shouts *Style* louder than your autograph. You'll be besieged again and again by well-wishers and autograph-seekers desperately seeking a piece of you. Remember, the artifact you create will be a family heirloom proudly displayed, often under glass, for generations to come. In a few seconds, you are creating a treasure for posterity.

So, *think* about what you're doing!

A lounge singer's autograph jumps off the page. It leaps like Michael Jordan before the eye. Its graceful swoops and swirls excite and stimulate all of the senses. To see Wayne Newton's autograph is to hear him sing again, to smell the Arabians.

Make your autograph big. Make it soar. Make it larger than life—almost a landscape. Make the capital letters spinnakers before the winds of fame. Make it important. Make it a Rorschach test.

A lounge singer who gives a small autograph disappoints a fan. As the signature shrinks, so shrinks the man, the wardrobe, the talent. A tiny autograph is a

stingy, heartless thing. Don't cheat your public. Give
your best when you sign. And make sure there's ink in
the pen.

BUD E.'S STYLISH TOP 10

Milton Berle, if you're reading this, allow me to say
something personal. When it comes to Style, you, Sir,
stand alone. The word *legend* doesn't begin to encompass
an individual of your girth. You discovered me. You
taught me everything I know. Your profound influence
on our industry has been felt for more than eighty years
and will be felt for eight hundred more. On behalf of the
thousands and thousands of people whose careers you've
helped, I salute you. You're the King. And the greatest
Uncle anyone ever had.

Now, let's pause and reflect for a moment. Let's consider some of the other leaders, the trendsetters and Mon-
archs of Style. Yes, the list is controversial. It includes
people from all walks of life. But Style, like everything
else, is about choices. Allow me to share with you a list
of people whose choices have set them apart:

1. LIZ TAYLOR. Throughout all the marriages, the
surgeries, the weight gains and losses, she has kept
her crown firmly set on her breathtaking hair. The
violet eyes, the cleavage, the emeralds, the gowns,
the choice of attorneys. Who does it better? A dear,
dear friend.

2. PABLO PICASSO. He turned everything he
touched into commercial art and got top dollar for

it. From gallery to gift shop to museum hallway, his work unleashed wave after wave of Style. I have several at home. How many guys can get laid at eighty with a paintbrush and a pair of baggy shorts?

3. XAVIER CUGAT. Cartoonist, bandleader, restaurateur. The man did it all. The glasses, the pencil mustache, the *va-va-voom* rhythms, the chicks on both arms—unmistakable. The worst putter ever. I kidded him, I loved him. Coogie.

4. DOLLY PARTON. Bright, sensitive, prolific, gracious. Too often the butt of jokes. You won't read any here. I've had it *out to here* with those jokes. We've worked together, written together, shopped together so many times. I've come to trust Dolly's unerring eye for fashion. And wigs? Wooo! The Best.

5. PRINCE CHARLES. Pure class. The understated men's suitings, the simple silk ties, the ears pinned back. Always appropriate for a Royal.

6. JACQUELINE ONASSIS AND JACQUELINE BISSET. My "Jackies." The epitome of understated class and sex appeal. I wish Jackie "O" could have had a screen career. I love what she's done with the publishing thing. As for Jackie "B," she's always been the First Lady in my book. Thanks, "B." You're invited back to the ranch anytime.

7. JOHN FORSYTHE. Silver locks, dignified demeanor, a seemingly endless television career. From "Bachelor Father" to whatever he's doing today, simply the best father figure on the globe. Great set of pipes, too.

8. JOHN GOTTI. No, I don't approve of *everything* in his background. But when it comes to courtroom attire, the Dapper Don does it best. The peacock chest, the double-breasted look—perfect. Can't wait to see the jailbird suit.

9. DYAN CANNON AND ANN-MARGRET. How do you pick between them? The figure that ate New York, and the legs that knocked out Elvis. We've served on so many boards together. Ann's a great cook. And who but Dyan could keep Cary Grant young?

10. MRS. RAY KROC. Wife of the founder and chairman of McDonald's, the fine food empire. A lady of great vision. Her recycling thing swings the most. I want the account—badly.

T H R E E

Dressing

The babes can't take their eyes off me.
Why?
Wardrobe, my friend.
Material means more than song selection.
Allow me to share my philosophy.

DO CLOTHES MAKE THE MAN?
YOU BETTER BELIEVE IT!

The Bible says it best. In the Garden of Eden, Adam and
Eve—the original swinging cat and kitten—hung out in
the nude. Fine. Look what happened. The apple thing
went down, and *boom*. Adam's career was vamoose. It
didn't start to turn around until he got the fig leaf.

YOU OUGHTA BE ME

THIS CUSTOM-MADE JACKET HELPS ME BEAT THE
ODDS. THE CONCHO BELT WAS A GIFT FROM MY GOOD
FRIEND JIM MORRISON. EVEN WHEN YOU'RE BEHIND
ME, YOU KNOW WHO'S WEARING THIS ONE.

That was the turning point—the fig leaf.

With the leaf, Adam gained something. A sense of confidence, a sense of control, a sense of mystery. He could lay back a little, be understated, not blow it all up front.

It drove Eve nuts. He started humming a little. She started paying him ... in kumquats, apples, whatever they had around.

DRESSING

41

It was the dawn of lounge singing—all made possible by wardrobe.

From these very crude beginnings, mankind has stretched the limits of lounge singing. And naturally, fashion has moved forward, developed, come to the very forefront and become a cornerstone of the entertainer's art.

Elvis in his jumpsuit—legendary. Despite the fact that it was polyester in fabric, it was inspired in design. Trendsetting. Fantastic. The sideburns exploded against the high white collar.

Lounge singers, remember: Clothes make the man. It's all about threads, baby.

GROOMING:
THE TAN AND THE MANICURE

I think George Hamilton said it best. We were poolside at the Beverly Hills Hotel. My cabana. He's charging drinks to my bungalow like a bandit. We're sunning. I've got some nice color coming. Frankly, George was looking a little like a wallet. But he turned to me and said: "You know, Bud E., you can be too rich and you can be too happy, but you can never be too tan." I'll never forget those words, even as I jot a get-well card to George after facelift number three.

The lounge singer has a place in the sun.

Why?

Because a healthy glow goes hand in hand with Talent. In fact, *tan* and *talented* share the same first two letters. Coincidence? Perhaps.

What does the tan say? The tan says, "I have free time," "I get outside," "Join me poolside." The tan suggests the fantasy of the singer with his (or her) shirt off, bronze muscles glowing in the sun. It suggests youth, athletic vigor. It brightens the teeth, enhances charisma. As a budding lounge singer, you must commit to your tan.

Should you use a tanning salon? Absolutely, although the color of the salon tan pales in comparison to the hue of a poolside tan. I have used salons effectively in the winter at Lake Tahoe and Atlantic City. But a poolside suntan is a classic for good reason. Maybe it's the chlorine. Maybe it's the company. Maybe it's the oil slick from your fellow bathers. The color is unmistakable. It spells *L-E-I-S-U-R-E* in capital letters.

For those who are concerned about the quote-unquote ozone problem, allow me to suggest Bud E. Luv's Oze-Off Bronzing Cream, a delicate salve designed to give you peace of mind at poolside. Send $15.95 to House of Luv, Box 711, Las Vegas, Nevada 85103. No checks, please.

Now, to the hands. The manicure. I can't stress enough the importance of a good cure. The entertainer's hands are an extension of his soul. Do you want your soul to have a hangnail, a ripped cuticle, or a subcutaneous infection?

Do you want your bejeweled rings living next door to mangled nails?

No. You take care of the hands. You moisturize them. You polish them. You appreciate them ... or you invite trouble.

I remember years ago, Liberace and I were going

through his garage looking for the parts to an old candelabra. He tore a nail. It happens. He's human. But he ignored my advice to make an emergency appointment for a manicure at my favorite salon in Vegas, Ching Kow Pan Nails.

He went onstage that night wearing the boa. In the middle of "Flight of the Bumblebee," in an especially demanding passage, the boa got caught in the broken nail. The fingers were flying. Suddenly, there were feathers everywhere. One of them caught fire in the candelabra. Up went the boa. The smoke alarms went off, the sprinklers kicked in. The fire marshall was onstage like a shot, crawling over the red, white, and blue Rolls. The entire audience was evacuated soaking wet. Gross receipts of over $180,000 were refunded to irate customers. Bill Harrah was furious. The car was a total loss. All because Lee failed to get a manicure.

Need I say more?

YOUR VALET: MORE THAN A YES-MAN

Every lounge singer needs help. Personnel. Staff. You must have a manager, an agent, an attorney, a musical director, an accountant, a lighting director. Sometimes the list (and the payroll) seems to go on forever.

But at the heart of the lounge singer's staff is the valet. He makes choices no one else can make. He makes decisions too delicate to be left even to the entertainer himself.

His is a lonely existence.

MY TRUSTED VALET
LEON AT HOME . . .

SUSAN MUNROE

AND AT WORK.
T A DIFFERENCE
CE MAKES.

Leon has been with me for twenty-five years. He's family. Sometimes we spend hours together without uttering a word. Yet he knows me like a book. His delicate sense of color blows my mind. What he's *forgotten* about French cuffs could fill Versailles. The man is a mensch. His eagle eye for fashion has guided me all these years like a compass.

Imagine the pressure of serving a star like Elvis, Sammy, Frank, Tom, or myself. Imagine dealing with the constant barrage of things to be done: The pants that must be pressed; the shoes that must be polished; the jewelry that must be buffed to catch every ray of light onstage; the medication that must be dispensed at appropriate times.

You trust your valet with your makeup and your life. He must be tactful yet candid, soft-spoken yet forthright, delicate yet strong. Strong enough to pull the trigger on the .38 he's packing.

Did I say .38? Yes, I did. Your valet not only needs to know fashion, he needs to know firearms. Don't be naive. Trouble can come when you least expect it. If you're ever caught in your dressing room with your pants down, and an armed intruder enters, leave it to your valet to get the wrinkles out. And don't worry, he knows a good lawyer.

The Right Hair:
Rug, Plug, Caesar,
Scramble,
or Handicap?

Hair. Oh, my God, people! What is this I see on your heads? Ouch! What mental processes are taking place here?

Allow me to digress. Can I say mammal? What does mammal mean? It means hair. H-A-I-R. We're mammals, right? We have hair, right?

Some of you act like this is news.

Come on, people. Focus.

If you have hair, don't treat it like a dreaded relative visiting your scalp. Respect it. It makes you who you are—a mammal.

Groom it. Take care of your hair. Don't write your name in it. Don't cut it like a hedge. It's not shrubbery. Don't paint it blue. Don't tease it to death. How would *you* like to be teased to death?

Your hair is a living, loving extension of you. It's a fleet-footed messenger running, flowing, flying out before you, telling the world who you are. It's saying, "Hello, I just got out of bed" or "Good evening ladies and gentlemen, let's swing."

What your hair says is up to you. But whatever it says, it should say it *loud*.

Make your hair significant. Use lotion, mousse, spray. Use petroleum-based products if you have to. Give it depth, dimension, sangfroid, loft. Create levels. Choose colors decisively. And for God's sake, lose the *gray*!

DRESSING

47

LET'S FACE IT—I'M HAVING A GREAT HAIR
DECADE.

SUSAN MUNROE

Now, let's stop right here. A lot of people come to me and say, "Bud E., the advice is fine. But what about *me*?"

They lower their heads, and I see the reflection of my own perfectly coiffed hair in a shining dome that once was home to a healthy set of locks.

This irony always tears me apart. I know I'm talking to someone who will never have a good hair day.

But there's hope.

It can be different.

It can be fixed.

It can be purchased.

As the swallows return to Capistrano, so, too, can hair return to your head. It may not be your hair. It may not be hair at all. But you will have a voice again.

Don't delay, and don't skimp. Buy a lot, and buy it now. Don't be afraid people will notice you're wearing a piece. They will. Who cares? What matters is that you can still do TV.

The hairpiece, the toupee, the rug. Call it what you will. But if done correctly, a career is saved, tragedy is averted. Most important, the chicks, and your self-respect, are back.

The fit is critical. Try the George Burns Test. If you can fit a #4 Antonio & Cleopatra cigar between the nape of your neck and your rug, it's too big. Size down.

Color—all important. Match your piece to whatever existing hair you still have. If it's gray, dye it.

Try to make the texture as natural as possible. Avoid the chocolate-pudding Bob's Big Boy look. Keep the texture lifelike, the tempo lively.

Have several styles. Have several toupees, for that

matter. And pay top dollar for all of them. But remember, first and foremost, purchase a top-quality glue. Wind is your enemy. No one wants to see their hair on the ground. The broad you're with doesn't want to chase your rug around the tennis court.

Now, let's talk about plugs.

"Strangers in the night . . . scooby dooby dooo . . ."

It was right after I'd written that song for Frank. We were in the studio when he told me, "Mia hates the rug. What do I do?" I had him call my close, close friend, hair surgeon Donald Polyopolis. He was at the cutting edge of hairplug technology at the time. I knew Frank would love him.

Of course, they hit it off. And the next thing I knew, Frank had a new look, a new love, and another hit record I wrote for him. Pretty soon, everyone was doing it— some with more success than others. But it was something new, and I'm proud to say I helped pioneer the acceptance of plugs.

Hairplug technology has improved so much over the years that many of my doming friends are back in the thick of things. God bless them.

And now for the Caesar and the Scramble. Both of these travesties are trademarks of the tragic, disillusioned entertainer who thinks he has enough hair to work with, but doesn't. This deluded being will stretch the few sad strands of hair he has left in any direction on his scalp, hoping to retrieve his youth, hoping to create the *illusion* of hair. He is sadly mistaken. He's fooling himself. This is a battle that cannot be won. It's a hair Vietnam.

With the Caesar, all of the remaining hair at the back of the head is aggressively pushed forward, across the dome and onto the forehead. If you're lucky, you get the wispy, mockish little bangs. And what have you created? Do you really think you look like a Roman emperor? Who are you, Domus Eggulus? Do you hear the chicks speaking Latin? If you must resort to the Caesar, buy a lot of grapes, and plan to eat them alone.

Wake up, Eggulus! You look ridiculous! Do yourself a favor—put a rug on that marble floor.

The Scramble is another nightmare.

The Scrambler begins by growing ten inches of hair right next to his ear—*on one side only!* He meticulously parts it just above the ear, then combs the rest straight across to the other ear. Like a New York–Tokyo flight crossing the North Pole. Fine, if you want your head to look like an airline route map.

Are you listening, Don Rickles?

I kid Don. He's nuts about me.

The *creative* Scrambler combs the strands in a circular pattern, like the trade winds, creating a dizzying effect.

What happens in the wind? I'd rather see autopsy photos. Without spray, the hair is suddenly airborne, standing straight out from the head ten inches—revealing a blinding dome. Everyone's running for cover. *With* spray, and I mean several cans, the entire hair mass hinges off the scalp like an open cockpit. It's a hairline flight *you* don't want to be on.

If you choose to Scramble, get ready to gain thirty pounds. *Because you're never going outside again.*

You're never going anywhere. You're a shut-in.

Guys, wise up. Smell the java. Get a rug. Or get plugs.

Finally, there's what I like to call the HandiCap. It's the cheapest and quickest way to cover insufficient hair. Put a *hat* on it. But it doesn't work in the lounge unless you're Hank Williams, Jr., or Johnny Lee. It's disrespectful. The only time the HandiCap is justified is in the morning hours—to hide morning hair.

PRICING HAIR: WHAT TOUPEE?

If you aren't paying at least $6,000 per hairpiece, you're cheating your public and fooling yourself. This is your career we're talking about. Buy it on time if you must. The hairpiece stands at the summit of your persona. It's the crown. Are you going to be the King or a Joker?

WHAT TO WEAR

Now that your head is covered, let's cover the body—in fabric. Quality fabric. You should be wearing the best the garment industry has to offer. Your clothes are an extension of your personality and your pocketbook. Like your reputation, they precede you. Your audience sees what you're wearing before they see you. So lose the clown outfit!

Your clothing must dazzle. It should shimmer. But more important, it should set you apart from the little

SUSAN MUNROE

THIS RICHARD
TYLER CLASSIC,
NOW IN THE
SMITHSONIAN,
WILL BE MOVED TO
THE BUD E. LUV
MUSEUM IN LAS
VEGAS.

ANOTHER RICHARD
TYLER CLASSIC.
CHICKS REALLY GO
NUTS FOR THIS ONE.

SUSAN MUNROE

people, the people in your audience. If you're in the audience, do you want to look up and see a guy onstage wearing what you're wearing? No. The Gap is closed. You want to see an icon, a legend, a fashion fantasia.

Whether it's a blazer, a tuxedo, a finely crafted shirt, or a pair of hand-sewn Italian shoes, it should scream *expensive!* If the audience looks at your clothes and sees less than five figures, you're sunk. You're a fashion *Titanic.*

You want the broads to go nuts for you, right? You want them in a trance? Then hypnotize them with your clothes. Weave a spell with your threads. Tantalize.

You don't have to be Einstein to understand $E = mc^2$.

Entertainment equals money and chicks squared.

But you'll never get the money or the chicks without great hair and great clothes.

NATURAL FIBERS VERSUS SYNTHETICS

It was 1858 when a gooey black substance was discovered in a lake somewhere in western Pennsylvania. Soon the whaling industry was beached. Petroleum was born. The next thing we knew, it was burning in fires around the globe, heating homes, moving produce to market.

Unfortunately, by the mid-seventies, it was also heating the armpits of lounge singers and moving artificial fabrics to market.

Artificial? Yes. This miracle substance had a sticky dark underbelly. It allowed cheap blends to exist. Your

50–50s, your 60–40s. Your Poly-Dacron blends. It purged a nation of its character.

Of course, the synthetics didn't need ironing. No one wanted to touch them. Polyester made a clown of the president, a laughingstock of the papacy. It devastated the business community. Housewives broiled in it. Children suffered under its smothering influence.

And just to bring it home, lounge singers were trapped, too—trapped in a garment that should have been a gallon of high-test. The performers were uncomfortable, and so were their audiences, watching them sweat like pigs.

Natural fabrics were thrown in a corner. Cottons, silks, woolens were hidden, neglected by a generation. Forgotten.

Then the tide began to turn. And I like to think I may have had a little something to do with it.

I was working with Wayne Newton at the Frontier. I was wearing natural fabrics. He was in the polyester jumpsuit, the one with the big belt. He was losing twelve pounds per show. I was holding my ideal weight. I never broke a sweat, even during the dance routines.

When Wayne came offstage, he needed a squeegee.

Wayne turned to me and said—and I'll never forget this moment—he said: "Bud E., how do you stay so cool?"

I showed him my labels: 100 percent cotton, 100 percent virgin wool.

His eyes lit up like a Vegas jackpot.

The next night, *Wayne was wearing wool.* And cotton. Cool as a cucumber.

His high notes were clearer. His performance sharper. His Arabian horses more disciplined.

And so it began.

Sammy, Dean, Tom Jones, Jack Jones, Grandpa Jones, "Me and Mrs. Jones"—everybody was hopping back into the Naturals, torching their doubleknits. I sold my Exxon stock. I made a killing in sheep and cotton futures. Silkworms came back.

The rest is history.

If it doesn't say 100 percent cotton or 100 percent virgin wool, it's 100 percent bogus. Be fair to your audience. Be good to yourself. Keep it natural.

A brief word of caution concerning silk. Silk is an unforgiving fabric, a tyrant. Never wear a silk shirt onstage. It doesn't breathe. It's hotter than polyester.

Silk *blows*.

HARRY BELAFONTE SYNDROME

Daaaaaaaaaayy-O!
Dee-say-day
   dee-say-day-
      dee-say-day-
         dee-say-day-
            dee-say-daaaaaaaay-O!

Navel hair.

Why?

Because the shirt was allowed to be worn without the benefit of buttons.

A mere oversight? No. I loved what Harry was trying to do. It was an offshore attempt at style, manliness, calypso panache. Not bad.

But the shirt became a distraction from his enormous talent. *Hairy* Belafonte.

And no medallion!

Enough chest may be shown to provide an appropriate backdrop for the medallion. Jolson loosened the black tie. Tom Jones removed it and opened his shirt. You saw the medallions. Fine. But disco's dead. Button up!

You're a lounge singer. A class act with dignity, not a stripper. Undress *after* the show, with the babe of your choice. Don't tally your bananas onstage.

THE MAGIC OF PANTS: THE TOM JONES STORY

A young man came to me from the Isle of Wales with a song in his heart and a handful of shillings in his baggy pants. He had a great set of pipes. Good-looking kid. He said he wanted to be in show business.

His name was Tom Smith.

I said, "Tom, it'll never work." I changed his name. To Jones. And the rest is history.

I wrote a few songs for him. Then we worked on the stylization of the act. The open shirt. The tight pants. The cucumber. It was too much. We went back to the cotton-sock look, and he soared with it.

TOM JONES BELTS IT OUT. NOTICE HOW HIS
PANTS SAY "I AM MAN, HEAR ME ROAR."

YOU OUGHTA BE ME

Chicks flocked. In droves.

The reason? *Pants.*

Choose your own pants. Pleated. Pegged. Baggy. Flaired. Full-cut. Then add what you will. A belt. Rhinestones. A satin lining. But always make sure the pants flatter you. Ask yourself: How do they feel? Do they pinch, bite, ride? Do they cling? What do your pants *say* about you?

Always remember the *Second* Rule of Show Business: Your pants should be so good they can do the show without you.

FOUR

Jewelry: A Few Pointers, My Friend

Lounging well is the best revenge. And there's no more resplendent or satisfying way to lounge than in the company of fine gems and jewels.

Jewelry is a symbol of royalty. When you think jewels, you think the Crown Jewels, the pope's ring, the

Godfather's ring. Jewelry, extracted from the grit of the earth, cut and polished to a lustrous sheen, is a sign of success, power, and achievement. And it's more.

Jewelry is the lounge singer's Congressional Medal of Honor. Each ring, medallion, bracelet, watch, and pin signifies a battle fought and won at great cost and sacrifice.

I wear a diamond pinkie ring given to me by Conrad Hilton, Sr., in recognition of a rainy evening in October of 1972, when I did three shows in one night at the Vegas Hilton. I didn't get paid for the third show. It was a special, added performance for Mr. Hilton's mother.

The agreement was struck, man to man, backstage in the wings, moments before showtime. There was no paper. All Mr. Hilton had to say was, "Bud E., can you get me out of a tight squeeze?" And all I had to say was, "Of course, it's on me."

YOU OUGHTA BE ME

The next morning at 9 A.M., the ring arrived in my suite—inscribed. A beautiful four-carat VVS-1 diamond, G in color, encircled by twelve perfectly matched emerald-cut rubies.

It came with a magnifying glass. The engraved inscription read as follows: "To Bud E. Luv—For outstanding excellence in the performing arts and with deep appreciation from everyone in the Las Vegas entertainment community. With warmest fond wishes, Mr. and Mrs. Conrad Hilton Senior."

I cried.

Service. Pride. Emotion. Tears.

Jewels are my children.

THE LEGACIES OF SAMMY DAVIS, JR., AND LIBERACE

I can't look at any of my rings without thinking of Sammy—*Sammy Davis, Jr.*

He did for jewelry what Edison did for the light bulb. Sure, they laughed in the beginning. But they had to come back. Sammy had the power—the power of jewelry.

He was a dancing jewelry store, a Tiffany window. A singing showcase of diamonds and gold.

Ostentatious? Absolutely. Over the top? Of course.

Yes, the critics snickered. But Sammy wasn't wearing the jewelry for himself. It was for the common man (and woman)—people who couldn't own it, wouldn't own it, were afraid to own it. The couple married thirty years who couldn't afford a ring, couldn't even afford to come see Sammy. The jewelry was for them. Sammy flew them in, gave them a suite, and put them in the front row so they could see each and every ring. He lived to see the sparkle of his diamonds in their eyes.

They cried.

I only saw Liberace cry once.

Liberace was possessed by jewelry. He worshipped it. He didn't keep his rings and baubles in a safe, like the rest of us. No. He kept them in a fireproof altar. Some said he even performed religious rites with them. I don't want to get into that.

I went to see Lee at the Riviera. He was playing the main room with the dancing waters, the Rolls, the whole kit and caboodle. I'll never forget it. The memory is as clear as a freshly cut sapphire.

But there was something hollow in his performance—like an empty grain silo. He was *hoarding* his jewelry, *lording* it over his audience.

I went backstage, and I told him straight out: "Lee, you've got to let go of the jewelry. You've got to share it." And then, I gave him the line: "See these rings? Aren't they beautiful? Enjoy them, because *you* paid for them."

He cried.

These men—Sammy and Liberace—left a legacy of caring, a history of sharing. God rest their souls. I loved those cats.

ALL THAT GLITTERS IS GOOD

Just last week, I was over at the Excalibur checking out some new kids in the lounge, watching them do their thing and digging them doing it. Except for one thing. The lead singer was wearing a ring that looked like it was polished with a Hershey bar.

Maintenance, people. *Maintenance*!

A glittering jewel enters the room before the man (or woman) who's wearing it. The sparkle, the glow, the glamour must rule. It must shine like a star student in a spelling bee.

Clean, buff, shine, and polish—*hourly*. Let the jewelry blaze. Don't let your jewelry starve for attention. Oxidation occurs every 23.7 minutes, people.

And never use an abrasive cloth. Use a ruby cloth. Try the Bud E. Luv Ruby Cloth. $15.95. House of Luv. You know the address. No money orders, please.

HOW MANY CARATS IS ENOUGH?

Ten.

Twelve.

Fourteen.

Eighteen.

Twenty-four.

I'm sorry, my friend. You can't buy, own, or wear too many carats.

When we speak of the stones that adorn the lounge singer's hands, we're not talking Flintstones. Okay?

SUSAN MUNROE

THE WAYNE NEWTON COLLECTION.
HE'S SUCH A NICE NEIGHBOR. I WEAR
THESE IN HONOR OF THE
CHEROKEE NATION.

We're talking about gems of unparalleled excellence.

In diamonds, carat means size. And size is good. Are diamonds a girl's best friend? No! *Carats* are a girl's best friend. The old adage that size doesn't matter doesn't apply to diamonds.

How many carats should a diamond weigh?

How many you got?

Don't buy a jewel that's ashamed of itself. You'll just end up making excuses for it.

MEDALLIONS: A WAY OF BEING

The Bible. I'm nuts about it, sure. But it's been two, three thousand years since that stuff went down.

Remember the Samson and Delilah thing? The Bible says Samson gets the hair cut, and the strength goes vamoose. Suddenly, he's a ninety-eight-pound weakling.

But, hey. Do you really think it was the hair? No, no. It wasn't the hair. Samson took his *medallion* off— probably after a hot night in the tub with Delilah—and *boom!* The juice was gone.

We'll never know what image was on Samson's medallion, but we'll long remember the lesson: Your medallion gives you strength.

I gave Sammy his famous *S* medallion, emblazoned with diamonds. I gave Engelbert one with his last name on it: *Humper* on one side, *dinck* on the other. I gave Speaker of the House Tip O'Neill the gavel medallion, and Ralph Nader the one with the Corvair on it. It looked great with his Nehru jacket. Over the years, I've proba-

SWINGIN' WITH PETER GABRIEL. NICE MEDALLION.

bly received as many medallions as I've given, if not more. I treasure them all. I have one that was a personal gift from Pope John XXIII that's my favorite. It's embossed with a lifelike portrait of St. Genesius, which I discuss a little later in chapter 7.

Why are medallions special?

The medallion is a way of being. It suggests vulnerability. It implies that the singer is not all-powerful, that there is some greater force than him or herself, to which he or she pays homage. Can I say homage?

The medallion is a dangling participant in the delicate alchemy of the lounge. It's a beacon. A beacon for prayer. It's also a beacon for broads.

The chicks go wild when they see a medallion sparkling beneath the folds of a 100-percent-cotton dress shirt. They come closer. They must be *near* the medallion. The brilliance attracts them like moths. They have to *touch* it. And in doing so, they have almost no choice but to touch you, the lounge singer.

Is this good news or what, Samson?

You don't need a pick-up line with a medallion. You need protection, and lots of it.

Let your medallion speak for you. Your address book will swell with chicks' phone numbers.

Collect medallions. Trade them. Give them to your friends.

But wear one. It's the best.

SUSAN MUNROE

THE LEGENDARY
BLACK OPAL RING
THAT FRANK
SINATRA AND DEAN
MARTIN GAVE ME
ON MY TENTH
BIRTHDAY. ALMOST
AS PRECIOUS AS
THE MEMORY
ITSELF.

STORIES BEHIND THE JEWELS: NOW THEY CAN BE TOLD

Allow me to pause and reflect on some of the fine jewelry I've been privileged to collect over several decades in this business we know and love called show.

I'll never forget the wrap party following the completion of one of the finest motion pictures to be produced in the history of the motion picture industry—*Ocean's Eleven.*

Unfortunately, my performances were left on the cutting-room floor due to union problems with minors. At any rate, let me say that the Rat Pack knows how to throw a party. And this just happened to be the greatest party in the history of Las Vegas. It also happened to be my tenth birthday.

I'd been writing some charts for Sinatra. I went over to the party. The Kennedys were there. There were broads everywhere. Joey Bishop had *two* on each arm. Frank was with one of the most beautiful blondes I'd ever seen.

The minute he sees me walk in the room, he has the Count Basie Orchestra break into the swingingest version of "Happy Birthday" ever blown. Out comes the cake—six towering feet of it. This broad pops out. She sashays over to me and puts her right hand out. I've got Frank on one side, Dino on the other. The broad hands me a beautiful velvet box. I open it and there's a gorgeous ring—a three-carat black opal surrounded by ten twenty-point clear-as-a-bell diamonds in the most spectacular setting that can be devised.

A hush falls over the room.

You could've heard an olive drop!

I've had this birthday ring sized several times as I've come of age. I still wear it to this day.

A few years later, the fellas and I had the honor of doing a command performance at Royal Albert Hall for the queen. She loved what we were doing. Prince Philip

OPERATION CARAT STORM—
WHAT I WEAR ONSTAGE TO WIN THE WAR.

SUSAN MUNROE

The Fabulous

BUD E. LUV

cronus

ABOVE: THIS IS WHAT I CALL MY DISCO ROLEX, CIRCA 1975. A THANK-YOU GIFT FROM BARRY WHITE FOR STARTING THE DISCO MOVEMENT.

LEFT: THE INFAMOUS LE COULTRE WATCH THAT HAYLEY MILLS GAVE ME. WHAT A SWEETHEART.

LE COULTRE

was finger poppin'. And I have to say Markey and Mikey never played better. It wasn't a union gig. We didn't care. We were there to wail. And wail we did—with all our might.

The queen sent word backstage that she wanted us to come to the palace the very next day to play high tea. What a great room. Acoustics: sensational. The gathering was small and intimate, and gave me an opportunity to mix and mingle. It was January. I wore ermine. The response was gratifying, but I didn't get my normal standing ovation. I wondered if we'd bombed.

Imagine my surprise when the next day at Claridges, a packet arrived. It was from the queen. I opened it. It was one of the Crown Jewels. Her Majesty had dispatched the chamberlain straightaway to the Tower of London to select a little something for the Budster. It was a ring that had belonged to Henry III, very historical. What a lovely gesture.

I had it melted down—it wasn't quite right for me—and reset the stones into something that really made a stunning piece. It always makes me think of the queen, and we still swap Christmas cards to this day.

My 1933 Le Coultre "Mystery Dial" watch was a gift from Hayley Mills. She was filming *The Parent Trap* when we met. Maybe it was the English accent. Maybe it was the full, pouting lips. Whatever it was, there was chemistry. I'll never forget those afternoons in her trailer. The inscription says it all: "Bud E., I luv what you do with what you have—Hayley." I wear this watch on the Summer Solstice every year.

Another very special piece of jewelry in my collection is my coin ring. The coin is a handsome striking from the Franklin Mint, in platinum, with a traditional portrait of Benjamin Franklin. It was a personal gift from Aretha Franklin. The coin is surrounded by diamonds, and the inscription on the band reads: "To Bud E. with R-E-S-P-E-C-T from Aretha." I gave Aretha a few tips on her early albums, helped her put a little extra *umph* in the rhythm tracks. She's nuts about me.

Even though I can't wear it, I'll always treasure one household item that I keep at the ranch. It's a crystal decanter with very special powers. But it's not your everyday crystal. It's a channeling decanter from Shirley MacLaine. By the way, she's had great legs for thousands of years. Shirley's a gas. Ask Nero.

SUSAN MUNROE

LUCKY IN LIFE, LUCKY IN JEWELRY. THIS IS MY RING OF FORTUNE—A DIAMOND THAT SPINS IN A ROULETTE WHEEL. BY I. FRIEDMAN & SON, 47TH STREET, NEW YORK CITY. PLEASE DO NOT TOUCH.

AS I USED TO TELL MY CLOSE PERSONAL FRIEND
WOODY GUTHRIE: "THIS LAND *WAS* YOUR LAND
BUT NOW THIS LAND IS *MY* LAND." HERE I AM
ON THE SITE OF THE SOON-TO-BE-BUILT BUD E.
LUV JEWELRY MUSEUM AND GIFT SHOP.

THE BUD E. LUV COLLECTION: PREVIOUSLY UNRELEASED PHOTOS

On the accompanying pages, I invite you to share with me several rare pieces from my jewelry collection that have never before been photographed. I carefully se-

BUD E. LUV MUSEUM & GIFT SHOP

lected these treasures because I thought you would get extra-special enjoyment out of them.

Please don't touch the photographs.

If you enjoy these photos, I have exciting news. The Bud E. Luv Memorial Jewelry Museum is slated to break ground in Las Vegas in December of 1995. The museum itself will feature displays of each and every piece of my jewelry collection in breathtakingly lifelike reproductions. I've personally designed the lighting. The security system alone will cost over $325,000. I've included a photograph of myself at the site along with blueprints of the floorplan. Mark your calendar and plan a special visit.

LIZ'S EMERALDS: A WORD OF CAUTION

Elizabeth Taylor—movie star, entrepreneur, legend, and a dear, dear friend. Who has eyes like Liz? Who has appeal like Liz? Who has husbands like Liz? She's dazzled her adoring fans for generations. She's *truly* one of the Hollywood Greats.

But like all of us, she's had her ups and downs. She's fought her battles with great courage. She's overcome hardship after hardship—weight gain, alcohol, drugs, men, and the anguish of aging—with style, class, and grace. And through it all she's found time to be a dedicated humanitarian, a champion of charitable causes, and a loyal friend to Michael Jackson.

However, I have a deep personal concern about some of Liz's jewelry. Let me be frank—it's the emeralds. We've all seen the pictures in *National Geographic*. The necklace, the stone—breathtaking. But I've seen them up close. We embraced at the Academy Awards several years ago. Liz, of course, looked marvelous. She kissed me on both cheeks. I looked down. And I knew.

Liz's emerald was not an emerald.

I prefer not to get into how this could have happened. I wish it weren't true. But I want you to benefit from this heart-wrenching experience.

When purchasing gems, remember these simple rules: Never go shopping when you're angry. Never buy gems when you're having a mood swing. And never purchase jewels your first week out of the Betty Ford Clinic. These are the rules, folks.

Your eyes can deceive you. Glass can appear semiprecious or even precious to the desperate shopper. Shrewd and unscrupulous salesmen the world over know this. They see the little white hospital bracelet on your wrist; they see the medications bulging in your jacket or purse, and they know. You're next, sucker.

As a lounge singer, yes, you should buy diamonds, sapphires, rubies, and emeralds. The *real* thing. Remember: Glass belongs in your limousine, not around your neck.

FIVE

What to Sing

People often ask me, "Why do you sing songs like 'Danke Schoen,' 'Y.M.C.A.,' 'If I Had a Hammer,' and 'It's Not Unusual,' in the same show?" Simple. Because I wrote them! But I'm getting ahead of myself. Allow me to pause and reflect on some of the musical trends I've created.

Time marches on, beats change, feelings change. Sometimes the tempo of the times is a slow waltz. Sometimes it's a samba. Sometimes it's a *ka-chow, chow, chow,* up, up and away kind of thing. Suddenly, the kids want something fresh. It's got to be *new.* It's got to be *different.* And as a lounge singer, you've got to roll with the punches.

Today, it's New Wave. Tomorrow, it's Permanent Wave. Or Rap. I'm currently working on a new album with my good friend, country superstar Porter Waggoner. We're combining country music and rap. We call it Crap. It's going to be fantastic!

But I'm getting ahead of myself. Again.

MUSICAL TRENDS: HOW AND WHY I CREATED THEM

I've been blessed in this career, which has spanned over three decades, with a knack, a penchant—can I say *penchant?*—a *gift* for creating musical trends. Folk. Rock. Disco. You name it, I've put my stamp on it.

For example, back in the late fifties or early sixties, something was blowing in the wind. I could feel it. I was hanging out at my ranch outside of Vegas. I had just stepped into the corral to ride one of my Arabians, and what do I find but some kids. Just sitting on the ground, legs crossed, eyes closed, humming, having one of those "be-ins," I think.

Anyway, they introduced themselves—Peter, Paul, and Margaret... Bobby Zimmerman and the Baez

THIS MUSTARD-COLORED
SUIT WAS A GIFT FROM
PORTER WAGONER UPON
COMPLETION OF OUR
COUNTRY-RAP ALBUM,
CRAP. LOOK FOR IT IN
YOUR RECORD STORES.

chick . . . nice kids. I *loved* what they were trying to do. But where's the *act?*

So, I invited them up to my Hospitality Area for a little barbecue. Next thing you know, we're sitting around the fire, strumming on a guitar that my good friend Andrés Segovia was kind enough to give me . . . just folks singing . . . and it hits me. Folks singing . . . *folk* singing! Who would have thought it would galvanize a whole generation and spawn an entire social movement?

Am I proud of it? You bet. Where would any of us be without such classics as "Michael Row the Boat Ashore," which I wrote at Lake Tahoe, or "Gumba Ya," which I wrote for Jilly Rizzo, or "Five Hundred Miles," which I wrote on the drive between Tahoe and Vegas?

The disco beat. *Tha-wump, tha-wump, tha-whump.* How did I come up with it? Let me explain.

I was in Paris on tour, working the Louvre. Wonderful art in that room, by the way. Standing O's. Encores. Crazy every night. Anyway, at that time, I never traveled in Europe without my Magic Fingers massage bed. So, when we arrived in Paris, Mikey and Markey carried it upstairs to my quaint, intimate suite overlooking the river.

That night after the show, I got in bed, dropped in about six quarters and *tha-wump, tha-wump, tha-wump*—the bed's everywhere! Markey had forgotten the voltage converter Edith Piaf had given me, and the bed was bouncing off the antique furniture like a Mexican jumping bean.

I was upset at first, then I thought . . . that beat . . .

**HERE I AM WITH FELLOW FUNKMEISTER
GEORGE CLINTON.**

that *tha-wump, tha-wump, tha-wump* ... there's something *new* there.

Disco was born.

When I think fresh, new, exciting and revolutionary ... Woodstock rushes to mind with a flood of memories. After organizing the festival (and, by the way, I never took a penny for it), I drove up to the site with

Bobby Darin. We took my Winnebago. Just to experience that sea of faces is something I'll always remember.

The weather was terrible. Melanie went overtime with the roller-skate medley. The promoter had to come to me and tell me *my* set was canceled. Imagine Bud E. Luv not playing his own festival! Darin and I were about to leave, disappointed we weren't going to get on the main stage, when our presence was urgently requested in the Bummer Tent. Of course, Bud E. never refuses a request, so we went.

The sight of those rain-soaked kids in that tent—the bulging eyes, the grinding teeth, the drool, the way their faces contorted when they saw me and Darin—it humbled me. And I thought Jerry's Kids had it bad! These young people were pathetic! And yet, being in the presence of those less fortunate than myself—and it's so easy to forget that so many are so much less fortunate than myself—I wanted to capture their hearts.

The kids were already freaking out when we got there, but when I started to perform, they really freaked out. I can understand why. I must have improvised a dozen songs on the spot—too many to mention—but fortunately Santana, Joe Cocker, Jimi Hendrix, Canned Heat, and many, many others were there to bear witness. They took those songs and flew with them. They soared with them. I'm so grateful for the magic of the motion picture camera that captured it all, captured the trend that was born that rainy day in the Bummer Tent at Woodstock. I always think of it as my favorite festival.

Okay, you're out of the warm-up suit. You're dressed. You're in your jewelry. You've stretched your talent. You've located your style. You're ready to musically ride that wave, reflect those times. What do you sing?

Fortunately, I can help.

Here's a little list of songs—a few of my personal favorites—that are surefire. I don't care what country you're in. It could be Israel. It could be Botswana. It could be the Midwest. I don't care. If you go onstage and sing these songs, you're going to kill. You're going to score. You're going to be an entertainer.

1. "Tie a Yellow Ribbon ('Round the Old Oak Tree)." I wrote it for Tony Orlando, but its appeal is universal.

2. "The Theme from 'Love Boat.' " Maybe it's the beat, maybe it's the lyric. Who knows? It works.

3. "Don't Go Changin' (Just the Way You Are)." I love what Billy Joel tried to do with it. Make it yours.

4. "I Feel Free" by Cream. It drives the chicks nuts.

5. "Strangers in the Night." When he was dating Mia Farrow, Frank wanted something to fuse their souls. I like to think I nailed it with this one. Try it with blue stage lighting.

6. "You'll Never Walk Alone." Pure theater.

7. "Ladies of the Canyon." Reminds people of when L.A. was a laid-back and gentle town.

8. "MacArthur Park." It took so long to bake it, but it cooks.

9. "Having My Baby." Gives the ladies an indelible mental picture of something they're all dying to do for you.

10. "Send in the Clowns." Always appropriate.

11. "When I Was Twenty-one (It Was a Very Good Year)." A song that ages like fine wine. So many people have recorded it, I sometimes regret having written it. Ricardo Montalban could have had a monster hit with it.

12. "Do Ya Think I'm Sexy?" If they don't think you're sexy, get out of the lounge!

13. "Mack the Knife." As a closer or an opener, there's none better. Dietrich used to love it when I did it.

14. "Me and Mrs. Jones." A must. Learn it, but beware of the high notes.

15. "The Windmills of My Mind." Larger than life.

16. "Danke Schoen." A little something I wrote for Wayne Newton. A beautiful sentiment—

and what more beautiful language to sing it in than the language of love, German?

17. "DISCO INFERNO." Although I have a bone to pick with The Trammps, who originally recorded it, the beat is irresistible.

18. "BOTH SIDES NOW." Joni wrote this after a weekend we spent together in Reno. There's something about the lyric that captures the magic of that time.

19. "WHAT KIND OF FOOL AM I?" This song I wrote for Sammy became his personal trademark. I think you'll enjoy performing it, too.

20. "COPACABANA." A by-product of my torrid affair with Lola Falana. It has the *umph* she had when she was young.

21–24. "IT'S NOT UNUSUAL," "DELILAH," "WHAT'S NEW, PUSSYCAT?" AND "GREEN, GREEN GRASS OF HOME." You, too, can be a stud singing this quartet of favorites from my Tom Jones Songbook.

For the rest of the songs on my Top 40 Hit List, send $15.99 in cash or money order to:

> House of Luv
> P.O. Box 711
> Las Vegas, Nevada 85103

People . . . please . . . no credit cards.

WHAT NOT TO SING

The lounge singer's repertoire is a rich cornucopia of treasures we refer to as songs. It should be spilling over with tangerines, mangoes, kiwis, and other diverse heavenly delights—a luscious treat for each and every member of the audience.

However, some songs spell death from the first note. Do I want to rain on anyone's parade or stifle the creativity of young singers today? No, of course, not. But my friends, take it from me—a wise lounge singer knows his (and her) limits.

How do I spell disaster?

Allow me to count the ways:

1. "YOU ARE THE SUNSHINE OF MY LIFE." Wrong. You're not. No one is. The lyric is a lie.

2. "NEW YORK, NEW YORK." The Chicago families who have a controlling interest in Nevada entertainment don't appreciate this one. Make friends, and leave this one to Liza.

3. "GUANTANAMERA." Unless you're in Havana, who's listening?

4. "FEELINGS." Keep them to yourself.

5. "MY WAY." Tough call, I admit. But let me try to explain it this way. Yes, it's a classic. Yes, my close personal friend Paul Anka wrote the music. Yes, I wrote the lyrics. But do *you*, the young lounge singer, really have the *dimension* of personality, the *charisma*, the *stature* to make this believable? I do. Frank does. *You* don't. Drop it.

6. "I FEEL PRETTY." I don't think so.

7. "SOMETHING IN THE WAY SHE MOVES." The Beatles? Ouch!

8. "MANDY." Careful. Manilow owns this one and, oy, what lawyers.

9. "YELLOW BIRD (FLY HIGH IN BANANA TREE)." Fly this. Need I say more?

10. "BALLAD OF THE GREEN BERETS." I've seen this one work under certain circumstances. For instance, I performed it once for General and Mrs. Norman Schwartzkopf at an exclusive dinner party in their lovely home. But there are so many families of POWs and MIAs in today's lounge audiences who live with this nightmare daily, this is a tale of American heroes best left unsung.

Remember, lounge singers, the key word that guides your choice of material is taste. T-A-S-T-E.

MICROPHONE TECHNIQUE: DO'S & DON'TS

The time was 1877. The man was Thomas Alva Edison, a fair lounge singer in his own right. But he was a nobody until he invented the microphone. Imagine the concept— something that could say everything that you said, but louder. Incredible. And a gift for which we're all eternally grateful. But it has taken years and years to master its use.

What is the microphone?

PRACTICE THIS POSE AND USE IT OFTEN.

SUSAN MUNR

The microphone is not a sex organ. The microphone stand is not a crutch. The microphone stand is also not a sex organ. The microphone cord is not a pet snake to be wrapped around the shoulders. (That's the job of a good *mink*.) Yet, time and time again, we see it in lounges everywhere . . . the abuse . . . can I say abuse? . . . of Mr. Edison's invention.

YOU OUGHTA BE ME

The proper use of the microphone begins with a simple word: *respect*. Tom, Engelbert, Sammy, Frank, Tony . . . *respect* the microphone. It made them who they are, and it'll make you whoever you are . . . but *louder*. So, respect it.

I know what you're gonna say: "But James Brown *licks* the microphone. Why can't I?" People, PEOPLE! Licking, swallowing, hurling, swinging, disgorging the microphone equals *short career*. Such tasteless circus tricks are not the mark of a professional. Nothing shows class more clearly than the proper handling of a microphone.

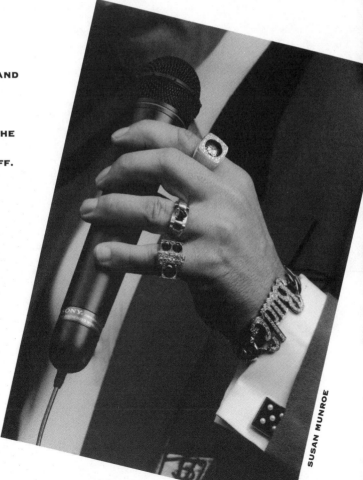

THE LOVE AFFAIR: A SINGER AND HIS MIKE. NOTE THE BRACELET WORN ON THE *OUTSIDE* OF THE CUFF.

SUSAN MUNROE

BALLAD HANDS. ALSO KNOWN AS THE
STEEPLE. IT SUGGESTS REVERENCE AND
HUMILITY, AND DRAWS PROPER
ATTENTION TO THE MANICURE.

SOME SAY THE LIMP
WRIST IS AN
EFFEMINATE SHOWBIZ
GESTURE. I SAY GO
FOR IT. IT SHOWS OFF
THE JEWELRY
BEAUTIFULLY.

Think of it this way: The microphone is a lady. Lady Mike, if you will. Treat her gently. Caress her. Compliment her. Sing to her, and she will sing in return . . . *louder*, yes, . . . but in return.

Remember these simple rules:

- Don't sing with the mike *in* your mouth.
- Always keep the pinkie finger on your microphone hand pointing up.
- Always thrust the mike away from your body for high notes—the "Finishing Thrust."
- Never hide the mike in your pants.
- Never give the microphone to a stranger during the show—you don't know where he's been.
- Hold the microphone in *one* hand, not two—you're not a monkey, and it's not a banana.

THE MASTER AT WORK.
MANY GET THE FACE RIGHT.
FEW GET THE FINGERS.

SUSAN MUNROE

SUSAN MUNROE

SOMETHING IN THE WAY
HE MOVES:
BUD E. LANGUAGE

"... You oughta be ... MeeeEEEeeeeEEEEeeee
EEEEeeeeEEEeeeeEEEEEE!"

Boom!

Applause. Standing ovation. Deafening applause. It
happens every night. It never fails.

YOU OUGHTA BE ME

Why?

Is it the lighting? No. The band? No. The clothes, the jewelry, the choice of material? To some degree.

The real answer, my friend: *Moves*.

Stage moves come from the soul. They emanate from within. They speak a language all their own. When a lounge singer is entertaining, *truly* entertaining, he communicates not only with his voice, his wardrobe, and his hair, but also with the movement of the corporeal frame itself.

WHAT TO SING

THE PONTIFF.
NOTE THE REVERENT PLACEMENT
OF THE HANDS AND THE
EXCELLENT EXPOSURE
OF THE RINGS.

A debonair shrug of the shoulders—what does it say? Arms reaching to the skies—what tale do they tell? Outstretched hands—what signal do they send?

Experienced pros—your Chevaliers, your Garlands, your Newtons—know the answers to these questions. They also know an audience will melt like cheese, not just at the sound but at the *sight* of their favorite entertainer.

Moves must be heartfelt, sincere, spontaneous... and soulful. They come from deep within.

Ray Charles came to me once and said, "Bud E., I don't seem to be communicating with my audiences. What can I do? I want people to feel my soul."

**THE BIG FINISH.
NOTE THE HEAD
HUMBLY CAST DOWNWARD,
THE MEDALLION
EXPOSED.**

I CALL THIS
THE MATADOR POSE.
READY TO TAKE ON A
RAGING BULL OR
EVEN *BE* ONE.

I told Ray to move. He was too stiff. We worked out a cute thing with the feet that Ray felt comfortable with. Then, we tried a little sway—back and forth—while he played the piano. And I told him to smile. It worked beautifully, and I've been so proud of what Ray's done with it. I'm sure something like this can work for you.

To get started, get yourself three full-length mirrors and install them in your rumpus room, your office, or your home dressing room. Spend a few moments getting comfortable listening to a Bud E. Luv tape or what have you. Start to feel the music. Experience the inner rhythm. Then let yourself go. Watch out for the mirrors.

People . . . no Elvis moves, please. The King is dead. Let his moves rest in peace.

Don't be an impersonator. Be an entertainer.

MEDLEYS:
ALWAYS AND FOREVER

Medleys are a lounge singer's bread and butter. And I'll tell you why. They're practical.

Medleys give the listener more tunes in less time. More hits per minute. More bang for the buck.

Sinatra, Luv, Newton, Jones—when we work, we only get fifty-nine minutes. Period. Or a guy named Guido is in your face talking about the unions, and believe me, the cat is *not* polite.

How on earth can we do all of our hits in fifty-nine minutes?

Medleys, man.

A medley isn't just a grab bag of songs thoughtlessly thrown together. A good medley has a theme. It has unity. A memory, an era, a feeling, a *thought*—any of these things can inspire a medley.

The songs must blend together seamlessly. For heaven's sake, don't just throw anything into a cheesy melee. You're not making an omelet. Think of it as a salad. Tempos must mesh. Themes must meld. Music must flow. The lyrics must be *friends*. Or at least acquaintances. A successful medley creates an almost overwhelming flood of nostalgia, pouring over the listener, transporting him or her back to wherever he or she was the first time he or she heard the songs. Sounds simple, right?

Let me give you a little example of a medley I'm working on right now. I'm constructing this one like a house. I call it my "People Medley." We start, of course, with "People," Streisand's signature song. Then "People Get Ready" right into "Everyday People," a little thing I wrote for Sly Stone, followed by "Flying Purple People Eater" in ballad tempo, then "Ah, look at all the lonely people." It'll go in the show right before "Surrey Down (To a Stone Soul Picnic)." Killer.

MEANINGLESS LIP EXERCISES

How many times have I seen the books telling singers to do this, do that, do whatever with their lips? Let me ask you, do you want to have a career? Then ignore anyone who tells you you'll be a better singer if you learn how to pout and pucker. It's bunk.

I saw it with the young Presley kid. He came to Vegas convinced the rock 'n' roll sneer was the key to his appeal. Every show, night after night, he worked the lip. Up, down. This way, that way. And to be very honest, some people may have enjoyed it. But look what happened.

Elvis developed carpal tunnel syndrome of the lip, virtually freezing it into that one-sided sneer. It was there at night when he went to bed. It was there in the cold light of dawn. Just knowing it was always there haunted him. He couldn't sleep. It led straight to the drugs. The rest, sadly, is history.

Was it worth it?

Even Sammy succumbed from time to time to lip abuse. But don't confuse lip motions with body language. Never the twain *should* meet. Lip movements are vulgar. Bardot made millions with them, yes, but she's a broad.

VEGAS THROAT: HOW TO DEVELOP IT WHEN YOU DON'T HAVE IT

Every profession has its trademark, its badge of honor. Construction workers have the rippling muscles that drive the chicks crazy. Tennis pros have those forearms. Attorneys have their $2,000 suits. Lounge singers have Vegas Throat. It's the hallmark of a pro.

The origin of Vegas Throat is simple. The dry desert air in Nevada dehydrates the vocal cords, causing a raspy sound. This can also lead to excess phlegm, which, frankly, can cause problems for some singers. I saw Tony

O. working one night at the Sands when he had a bad case. On the high note at the end of "Yellow Ribbon," he . . . well, Tony remembers. Enough said.

But what if you don't have Vegas Throat? What if you don't smoke (though most of the greats do)? What if your drinking isn't taking the toll on your voice that it could? Don't despair. You can develop Vegas Throat at home in your spare time with just a little extra effort.

Put a *de*humidifier in every room you're in during the winter. This will virtually eliminate all moisture anywhere in the environment. Without moisture, you're on your way.

If you don't smoke, invite a friend who does to ignite four or five packs of cigarettes or cigars and leave them burning in your presence. Ask him to blow smoke in your face. It may seem offensive at first, but it's excellent preparation for the atmosphere in the lounge. Now, take a deep breath and try to hit the Big Note on "My Way." Feel the burn?

Another way to get Vegas Throat: Gargle with salt. No water, just salt.

If all else fails, try screaming. At first, for ten or fifteen minutes a day, then gradually building up to twenty or thirty minutes a day. Now, some people say to me, "Bud E., I live in an apartment. I can't scream all the time." Fine. I understand. Allow me to recommend something.

Go to the nearest international airport. After picking the airline of your choice, go to the gate and ask the attendant to show you onto the tarmac, next to one of the larger jet airplanes. May I suggest that a small gratuity will work wonders here. Now, stand as close to one of the engines as possible, and sing the national anthem in full voice. Think of the engine noise as an unruly audience, and conquer it!

If you have to do this more than three or four times and still can't achieve the desired effect, you may have Orbison's Syndrome and should consult a physician.

RED THROAT LOZENGES: SAMMY'S BOO-BOO

Throat lozenges? Yes. By all means. But *never* red.

Let me explain why. The distressed throat cries out for relief like an orphan in the wilderness. There are many salves and balms. Gargling with warm water is good. Imposed silence. Rest. Hot tea with lemon, honey, and a nice Cognac back. A trip to the country with a quiet, sensitive chick who's not into talking. More rest. Throat sprays. And of course, lozenges. But not red.

I'll tell you a little story.

Something was wrong with Sammy. We all knew it. Everyone knew it. In the end, his fans knew it.

At the climax of every show, after a dazzling display of incredible talent, the Big Note would come, Sammy would open his mouth—and his fans would see red. Bright red.

Why?

Sammy was hooked. Hopelessly hooked on a generic brand of cherry throat lozenges.

Sammy allowed a cheap, over-the-counter package of candy to undermine everything the Candy Man stood for. He traded a fleeting moment of pleasure, secretly indulged in right before every performance, for the horror of a flaming red tongue that mocked his audience and almost destroyed his career.

I tried to talk to him about it on many occasions. We all did. We got nowhere. We tried red lighting. It killed the ballads. His valet tried red clothing. Sammy looked like a clown. We talked to Altovese. Finally, we tried a new tack. We all went to him—Dino, Frank, myself—and said, "Sammy, try the *lemon* lozenges." He wouldn't listen. It was too late.

It had to be cherry.

When it comes to throat relief, don't be color-blind. Stay with the flesh tones. Don't be fooled by flavor or garish packaging. Your career hangs in the balance.

SIX

Putting It All Together

Performing in the lounge is like going to dinner at someone's house. You take something: flowers, wine, a painting. A useful piece of furniture. You don't go empty-handed. If you're going onstage, bring something special, something extra. *Give* of yourself.

Now, let's stop for a second. Maybe you're thinking, "But Bud E., I have nothing to give."

I can understand that. When you're first starting out, when you're still in the limo with the training wheels, you can feel small. Insignificant. You doubt yourself. You wonder if you can pull it off. Everyone falls prey to these doubts.

It's only through patience with yourself, listening to the voice deep within, and medication that you emerge and take your first fledgling steps toward stardom.

Let's remember our basics. Style your hair (if you have it). Or put on the toupee—nice and easy. Don't forget the cologne. Slip into the dress shirt, the tuxedo, the cummerbund, the rings, the boots.

Now, let's ask ourselves these questions:

- Do you look talented?
- How's the charisma? Are the teeth clean?
- Are you walking like a celebrity? Is the Lateral Glide smooth, effortless? Good.
- Is your hair the best it can be?
- Do your clothes *feel* expensive?
- Jewels buffed?
- Are you *at one* with your medallion?
- Are your medleys ready to meld?

Good.

Now, take a deep breath.

In . . . . and . . . . out again.

Aaaaahh.

Feels great, doesn't it? See how you're beginning to feel lighter? There's a little bounce in your step now. All your hard work is about to pay off. You're ready to make *magic*.

That's right, magic.

You're going to weave a spell. *You're* going to mold the audience. *You're* going to phrase and emote. Stretch the limits. Conquer. Enter*tain*.

You're going to spread your wings and fly. You're going to knock 'em dead.

You're ready to go onstage, right?

Wrong.

WHO NEEDS PERSONALITY?
YOU DO, PUTZ!

You're about to make a big mistake. You're about to go in front of a firing squad without a last wish or a cigarette.

You've left home without it.

And I'm not talking about a credit card.

You've left home without the Big *P*—Per-son-ality.

Don't set foot onstage without it.

If you do, you're cooked. Finito. Kaputski.

Colonel Harland Sanders built a fried chicken business that swept the world. Chicken wasn't new. Frying wasn't new. What made his chicken soar? It wasn't the breading, the secret blend of spices. It was the way the Colonel looked, talked, and interacted with the spices and the chicken. The Colonel was *in* the breading. How? *Personality*.

It wasn't what he *did*. It's who he *was*. America could taste him on its fingers.

Spago restaurant in Hollywood, California, started with a man named Wolfgang Puck making pizzas. Any clown can make pizza, right? So why do the celebrities come night after night to this world-famous eatery? Lighting and seating, sure. But they come for Wolfgang—because he's *in* the pie. How did he get there? *Personality.*

Sure, you've got all the ingredients now—talent, style, jewelry, clothes, material, hair, makeup, microphone technique, moves. Fine.

But, people, we're *baking* here, not barbecuing.

We don't just throw ourselves on the grill like a slab of meat. We mix, we blend, we knead, we mold. Your act isn't an egg you carelessly crack open on a griddle to fry. It's a mousse—no, better—a *soufflé*.

Personality is the Mystery Ingredient. It's what makes Secret Sauce. It's the pinch of pimiento, the dash of oregano, the sprinkle of cumin that makes an ordinary recipe come bounding out of the bowl.

Look inside yourself. Listen to the inner voice. It's there. I promise you.

It's your personality.

It may be small and insignificant now. It may be choked, starved for air. Nurture it. Work with it. This is your pilot light. With it, you can set the lounge on fire.

Remember: Personality is the only genuine piece of magic any of us possess.

So here we go. It's coming now. Feel it? The real you is coming out. It's a beautiful thing. Now, you're ready to swing a little magic.

I *Love* What You're Trying to Do, But . . .

You're onstage, mike in hand. The band's cookin'. The clothes are perfect. Your hair looks like a million.

So, why the fire truck?

Okay. You're singing a medley of fire songs. Good. You want the macho image. Fine. But riding a hook and ladder? What are you, one of the Village People?

Personality expression, especially in inexperienced lounge singers, can go over the top. Youthful exuberance is a wonderful thing. But if taken to extremes, it can deflate the image. The Chairman doesn't sing from behind a conference table. Wayne doesn't come onstage in a headdress. They know who they are. They don't overdo it, and that allows the audience to see who they are.

You, too, can become understated with the following Understated Personality Exercise. Attend a foreign film; imitate the male lead; buy a trench coat and a pack of non-filter cigarettes. Now, go home to your family and mumble in subtitles. You'll be understated in no time.

Modesty and Sincerity: They Have to Ooze

I'm a legend. But I wouldn't be the legend I am today without modesty and sincerity. And I mean that.

Let's start with modesty. Modesty is the hallmark of a confident entertainer. It's essential. Being modest tells people that you know yourself, but you also know there's a Universe. You're a star. Yes. You're an almost constant explosion of dazzling fire. Yet you are humble. You recognize that there may be other stars. Other galaxies. Other lounges. You never forget your roots, your origins. You never forget the little people, the asteroids, if you will, who've swirled about you in orbit and made you what you are.

If you can't be modest, at least *act* modest. Study Southerners. They invented modesty. Say things like: "Gee, I don't know . . ." or "I hate to blow my own horn, but . . ." or "You're too kind . . ."

Look down at your shoes occasionally.

Use the word "little" frequently. If you've had a huge hit record, and I mean a *monster*, practice saying: "We recorded a little song a few years ago that we were fortunate enough to have a little bit of success with, and we'd like to do our little version of it for you now."

Show respect for your audience. When I'm onstage, I'm always polite to my audience. Even when I'd like to boil them alive in oil.

Use the royal "we" a lot. "*We*'d like to do a little song for you." "*We* hope you've enjoyed yourself." "*We* hope you'll come back and see us."

One of my favorite ways to close a show combines humility, respect, and a liberal use of the royal "we." It lets the audience know they come first. I say: "Ladies and gentlemen, we've played all over this nutty world. We've played high and we've played low. We've played on hallucinogens and alcoholic beverages. We've played for princes, kings, queens, popes . . . saddams. But *you* are unquestionably the best audience we've ever had."

I think Bob Dylan said it best when he said: "You've got to serve somebody." Your audience is your meal ticket. Serve them a scrumptious feast, not a taco.

Ask permission to say words. If the audience is especially delightful, and I want them to know they're delightful, do I just say "You're a delightful audience"? No, I ask permission. I say, "Ladies and gentlemen, you're a delightful audience . . . may I say delightful?" It makes them feel important.

You can do this, too. Ask whoever's around if you can have permission to say words. Then try it with your tux on.

I never forget my debt of gratitude to the many, many people—large and small—who've helped me throughout my career. The singers who have done my material. The audiences who have gone nuts for me the world over. The jockeys who've won so much money for

TODAY: FROM LEFT TO RIGHT, MARKEY LUV, BUD E. LUV, MIKEY LUV.

SUSAN MUNROE

me at the track. The limo drivers, hair technicians, parking attendants, croupiers, cocktail waitresses, pharmacists. The list is endless. I acknowledge them all. You should, too. Thank them for helping—whether they have or not. It makes you seem appreciative. Suddenly, you're modest.

Sincerity. So very important. Practice saying: "And I mean each and every word of this . . ." or "Ladies and gentlemen, believe me when I say . . ." or "I mean this from the bottom of my heart . . ." Get up first thing in the morning and practice these phrases. Before exercising, before coffee, before you put on your medallion. They'll become second nature in no time.

Okay, so let's review.

Did I say modesty and sincerity have to be present? No. I said they must *ooze*. Every pore. All the time.

Why do I say ooze? Because exploding is too much. Gushing isn't appropriate. Gushing suggests volcanic activity or geysers. The audience could get wet or burned. Exuding is too intangible. Feigning is morally wrong. Having an *air* of sincerity and modesty isn't enough. It's too airy. What's left? Oozing. Ooze it is. Ooze it must.

And never *attack* your audience. It's fine for comics. It's part of their act. It's not part of yours. You're there to transmit the wonder and majesty of song. You're Frank Sinatra, not Frank Gorshin. Don't be a wisecracking schmuck.

Okay, watch this . . .

You know friends, and I mean this sincerely, I'd be nothing without you, the listening and reading public. You've made me what I am—a legend, and a very, very wealthy man. I owe it all to you. And I'll pay it back . . . in diamonds.

See? It works, doesn't it? Didn't you feel important, just for a second? Of course you did. Was it oozing? Yes, it was oozing. Was it as good for you as it was for me? Yes, it was.

Remember: Your audience is there to give you money. Make them want to give you money. Be their servant. Buy them drinks. Fly them in from anywhere. Be humble. Humility and sincerity are good business.

WHAT TO FEED 'EM
ONCE YOU'VE GOT 'EM EATING
OUT OF YOUR HAND

I was singing at Valley Forge—a little engagement to celebrate the five hundredth anniversary of Columbus discovering America. I'm in the limo, in the warm-up suit, riding back to my suite at the Heritage Hilton. And I start to reflect. I'm reflecting on Ferdinand and Isabella. The king and queen of Spain.

How did Ferdinand get the broads? How did he snag Isabella? You've seen the portraits. What a blouseful! Why didn't she fall for the other kings? She could've had anybody. But Ferdinand *did* something, *had* something. Something irresistible, something that turned her on.

He had *class*.

Sure the other kings gave her furs, jewels, spices, all

that jazz. She was up to her wig in frankincense. But Ferdinand didn't just give her a new crown. He gave her a continent. He sent his valet, Columbus, out with three ships and said, "Don't come back without filling them up with gold." That's class.

If Ferdinand hadn't had class, there wouldn't be a New World. There wouldn't be a Vegas. No laughter. No music. Nothing. Just turkeys, Indians, and dust. Sad picture, isn't it? Anyway, back to Ferdinand. Munch, munch, munch. Ferdinand had Isabella eating out of his hand. How? Like we do in the lounge. By having class. He was a classy monarch.

So learn from the best. Get your audience eating out of your hand by showing some class. And once they're eating, feed them the finest there is.

What is this thing we call *class*? Class is hard to put your finger on, and it's hard to put on your finger. It shows itself in many ways. Here are some of the Hallmarks of Class:

- Accent
- Word choice
- Taste
- Manners

Accent. Don't talk like a slob. Talk like Peter Lawford or Sammy Davis, Jr. The broads will be falling over you three at a time. The way you pronounce words lets people know you have class. But remember, variety is the spice of life. Don't smother every word with your accent. You don't want to sound like Zsa Zsa Gabor or the Duke of Windsor. They bombed in the lounge. Pick certain words and make them your own by giving them flair. Sammy was great at it. He had the accent, yet he was still a hep cat. He could say "man," "my man," "my main man," and "dude" with the best of them.

Try this yourself.

Don't say *masterpiece*. Try saying *maaahster-piece*.

Don't say *show business*. Say *shay-o business*.

If you want a smoke, don't say *Hey, got a butt?* Try *Pawdon may, have you a cigar-ette?* Then say *Think-yew*.

Refer to the cats in the band as the *Oo-kiss-tra*.

Word Choice. The words you choose are important. Some words are a dead giveaway that you're a bum with no class. Use classy words like *attorney, car phone, venue, co-dependent, al fresco*. Most people won't know what you're talking about. That's fine. But they'll think you have class, and that's what counts.

HELPING SHEILA SPEND HER ALIMONY CHECK.

BLOWING THE AUDIENCE
A KISS IS ALSO A GOOD WAY
TO COVER UP A BURP.

Taste. Very important. Surround yourself with people and things that scream, *"I have good taste."* What is good taste? A Steuben glass windshield on your limo. A mother-of-pearl briefcase. A beveled glass clipboard. Sunglasses with your initials on them.

But it's more than just glass. It's little things—the color of your ranch house, your business card, your belt buckle.

Wayne Newton had a particularly handsome belt buckle made up a few years ago. It was 7¼ by 14 inches, roughly the size of a mailbox, carved out of silver, inlaid with turquoise and other semi-precious stones. It depicted the first Thanksgiving dinner with the Indians at Plymouth Rock. A simple scene and a simple piece, yet it proclaimed good taste.

I can't guide you in the choice of *all* of your accessories. Good taste is something you learn through observation and practice.

Now, to *manners.* Good manners are essential. If you don't display them, you won't be successful. Be hospitable. Be gracious. Be solicitous.

Here are some *don'ts*:

- Don't use another person's hand to cover your mouth when you sneeze.
- Never cook food during a performance.
- Don't ask strangers if you can take their medication.
- Don't make personal telephone calls during slow ballads.
- Never scratch anything in public.

Your Conductor:
He's Family

My conductor, Mikey Luv (no relation), is family. He's been with me for twenty-eight years. He's a monster! I discovered him in the Catskills at Harvey and Sonia Cohen's famed Catacombs resort. He and his brother, Markey, had an act. Mikey played accordion, Markey played clarinet. They weren't even eight years old but, man, could they blow. Imagine my amazement when I saw their name was Luv! I put them into my show and never looked back. The rest, my friends, is *histoire*.

Mikey's ability to read and write charts blows me away. He's like Isaac Newton with the apple thing. Unreal. He's the gonest cat that ever dug a groove. *Kachow?* He invented it. When we do "Surrey Down (To a Stone Soul Picnic)," and I see Markey pounding on the horn section to bring it up, I relax with a confidence that truly allows me to soar. He's a moose with the horns, a dog with the bones—the best in the business. And the dames that he rounds up after the gig—the choicest.

We've been through good times and bad. We added it up the other day. I've fired him 114 times, and he's quit 107. But through it all, we've remained brothers. This is what you want in a conductor—a man you can trust with your musical life. He must be a master of tempos, a musical bodyguard, a black belt in swing.

But you're saying, "Bud E., how on earth will I, a fledgling lounge singer, ever find a musical master with all of these qualities?"

It won't be easy, my friend. But it can be done.

Go to Times Square. It's crowded. There're people

everywhere. Fat ones, short ones, tall ones, thin ones, junkies, hookers, actors, narcs, lounge singers. Suddenly, in the distance, you see a little bald guy snapping his fingers. Maybe he has a mustache. Perfect. Whatever he's got, he's got rhythm. You can smell it, taste it. He could be your man.

Hire him. Buy him a tux. Get him a topflight orchestra and a baton. Work with him. Throw a chart in his face; see what he does with it. Does he swing? How's the smile? Is he cracking up at your jokes? Is he hip, yet subservient? Is he awkward in a slightly charming way? Is he doming? Cool. He's your guy.

Doc, Skitch, Paul, Mitch, Nelson Riddle, Les Brown—all wizards with a baton. I love these cats. We always have a blast at the Bud E. Luv Pro-Am Miniature Golf Classic, swapping jokes, swapping charts, swapping babes' telephone numbers.

Like them, your conductor should be a lifetime friend. He's the cornerstone in your musical edifice. Take him under your wing. Make him a confidant. Make him a partner. Make him family.

WHY YOU ALWAYS PAY THE BAND MINIMUM WAGE

But don't get carried away with the family bit. This isn't the Rockefeller family.

Remember: Your band works for you. You're a lounge legend. It's a privilege to work with you and be on your payroll. Thousands of cats would do it for free, right? So don't be a chump and overpay your band. Read my lips: *Min-i-mum Wage.*

Why? Simple. Paying more than minimum wage makes you look like a pushover. Like it's *not* a privilege to work for you. You look desperate, like you need their help. You should have the attitude that there are a million more cats in the alley where these came from—all dying to blow for you, the legend. If the band gets irate about their pay, slap them around a little. Or fire them. Who do they think they are, anyway? Paganini? They'll come back. Begging.

But I kid the guys. I haven't slapped Markey or Mikey in years. Haven't had to. Why? Perks and luxuries, my friend. That's right. The hidden benefits of working for Bud E. Luv—lavish gifts, special privileges, unexpected treats. I advocate philanthropy and generosity in chapter nine, "Becoming a Legend." *But I pay minimum wage.* So should you.

DEDICATIONS: THE PERSONAL TOUCH

You've just finished a song. The applause is dying. The room grows dark. The follow spot tightens. Suddenly, it's just the audience and your face, cameo-like in the darkness.

You step from the stage dramatically and move into the audience. It's time for something special, something personal. You look down at your belt. Is it time to undress? *No!* It's time for a *moment.*

It's time for a dedication.

Arlington National Cemetery attracts millions of people every year. Why? Because on each of those tombstones there's a simple dedication, and people *love* dedications. They come by the busload from miles around to read them in granite. Imagine how far they'd travel to hear one in the flesh.

I'm not saying that Arlington should be a lounge. Far from it. I love what they're trying to do there. I'm simply saying that dedications are a lounge singer's best friend. But you must practice, hone the craft, dedicate yourself to dedications.

There are four basic types of dedication—The General, The Celebrity, The Personal, and The Dead Guy.

THE GENERAL DEDICATION. This is also known as the "To All The Girls I've Loved Before" dedication. A necessity for the lounge. Perfect for conventions. "I'd like to dedicate this next song to all the orthodontists here tonight, as well as their lovely wives." When it comes to getting chicks, this is the drift-net approach.

THE CELEBRITY DEDICATION. It usually begins, "Ladies and gentlemen, there's someone very special in our audience tonight, a close personal friend. . . ." Then, you introduce the bigshot and dedicate the song. Don't worry if there aren't any major names in your audience. When you're starting out, any celebrity will do. Edd Burns. Billy Mumy. Orville Redenbacher.

Say something like, "Ladies and gentlemen, I'd like to dedicate this next song to a lovely lady who's with us tonight . . . Ruth Buzzi." It sounds great. And *always* mention that you're close personal friends.

THE PERSONAL DEDICATION. I like to bestow these upon the little people—noncelebrities in the audience who're having anniversaries or birthdays. This never fails with the broads. Before the show starts, your valet locates the best piece of ass in the house, finds out her name, and moves her to the front of the room. Before you go on, he tells you her name and where she's sitting. *Boom.* You do the dedication, look in her eyes, take her hand, and the rest is champagne and bath bubbles in the suite. If you don't score off a personal dedication, I'll refund the list price of this book. Write to: House of Luv, P.O. Box 711, Las Vegas, Nevada 85103. Enclose a photo of the broad.

THE DEAD GUY DEDICATION. Also known as the "Has Anybody Here Seen My Old Friend?" bit. Whether it's Marty Robbins, Bobby Darin, Franklin Roosevelt, or Walt Whitman, you can milk a lot of tears out of this baby. The key words to use here are *courage, vision, loyalty*, and *devotion*. Tell a personal anecdote. Tell a deathbed funny. Mention the last telephone call you received from the deceased. Close the dedication by saying that you still miss him very much.

If you have a day job, practice doing dedications at the office. Have the janitor turn down the fluorescents. Approach your secretary's desk dramatically, using a combination of the Entrance Gait and the Lateral Glide.

Oozing humility and sincerity, say, "Ladies and gentlemen, if I may, I'd like to take a moment to dedicate this fax of an unpaid invoice to a lovely lady who's with us this morning . . . a close personal friend . . ."

Then sing a medium-tempo ballad.

HANDLING HECKLERS

Hecklers represent an important, time-honored tradition in this business we call show. They add spice, verve, spirit, and danger to a performance. Don't let them scare you.

HEY, PAL,
LOSE THE POLYESTER
OR I'LL FLATTEN YOU.

A heckler is an opportunity.

Be thankful a heckler is in your audience, drunk, drooling, and demanding attention. Think of the heckler as a noisy infant. You're the parent. You have a chance to shine, discipline, dominate. By all means, respond to the heckler. A heckler ignored is a heckler forever. Think of him as a mosquito in the bedroom. Ignoring him won't help. Turn on the light and slap him.

I have an endless supply of snappy rejoinders that I use to demolish hecklers. And I'm happy to share a couple of them with you. For example, when a dame is heckling me, I say: "Sweetheart, I don't sit on the corner of your bed and talk when *you're* working." If it's an obnoxious guy, I may use this one: "Hey, pal, I don't bother you when you're trying to run the Slurpee machine at the 7-Eleven."

But don't ask for any more. Hire your own writers! Get your own wise guys with a typewriter. You'll be glad you did.

You can practice handling hecklers at home and at the office. Use your wife, your parents, or your boss. When your wife says, "Hey, honey, take out the trash," say, "You *cooked* it, *you* take it out." Rim shot. If your boss says, "Why are you late?" say, "I had to stop and buy some *carpet tacks* for your toupee."

The main thing is: Don't be overwhelmed by a heckler. You're in the driver's seat. He's a pedestrian. Squash him. The crowd will love it.

SEVEN

Making It in This Business We Call Show

"Sidney! My man! More coffee!"
How many times has he heard those words?
"Get me Wasserman on the phone!"
Sid's the best.
"Where the hell are those 8-by-10 glossies?"
Of course, he's the best, he's my manager.

"Where's my fountain pen?"

He's Mr. Las Vegas.

He's Sidney Moishe Rabinowitz. *Mr. R* to you. Sid to me. Always there. Never letting up. A pit bull on the phone.

SID RABINOWITZ:
A SALUTE TO MY MANAGER

I met Sid for the first time in the coffee shop over at Circus, Circus. I was seven. He was having the prunes and tapioca pudding. I was drinking coffee and smoking Larks. It had been a year since Mr. Berle had discovered me, and I was frustrated with my career. A week later, Sid and I struck a deal. He turned my career around. Since then, it's been smooth sailing—on the *Queen Mary*. Who could ask for anything more? *I* could! But I kid him.

I can't count the millions we've grossed together. The jets, the ranches, the threads, the broads, the miles of tarmac we've shared—Sid's been in for fifteen percent of all of it. I love the man . . . can I say love? Of course I can. Can I say mensch? You better believe it.

When I have a problem, personal or otherwise, I go to Sid first. He's like a wife—a wife with a big cigar. Sid, if you're reading this right now—and I know you are because you're writing it—thank you for thirty-seven wonderful years together. I have just one question: *Where's the TV series you promised me?*

Your manager is the Law of Gravity in your universe. He makes the money fall in your lap, and he keeps it from floating into outer space. You need him more than hairspray.

How can you spot a good manager? Listen for the gravelly voice. Check the cigar size. Is it unwieldy? Good. A huge cigar closes deals—no one wants that thing in their office for long. After ten minutes, they're signing anything to get the smell out.

Make sure your manager is thick-skinned.

And make sure he can *count*.

WHERE TO PLAY

Vegas, Vegas, Vegas. That's the key. Tahoe, Reno, Atlantic City? Darn tootin'. Tents, fairs, rooms, and lounges the country over? Yes, by all means.

But stay out of Holiday Inns.

Did you hear me?

You're not going to make the coin, the bread, the moolah in your little pretend lounges burping up Top 40 hits. Noooooooo. Bupkus. Zippo. Your average motel food and beverage director ain't exactly Ziegfeld. Capeesh? Lose him.

Choice of venue is critical for the lounge entertainer. If you can't play the main rooms or the established lounges, be creative. Take advantage of your home and work environment. Every company has an employees' lounge. Turn it into a *real* lounge. Have rheostats installed, and dim the lights. Remove light bulbs if necessary. Purchase tablecloths. Build a small stage in one corner. Buttonhole someone to be your maitre d'. You're ready to entertain. And the best part is, you're already

MELINDA PERFORMS GREAT TRICKS,
BUT I'VE GOT THE *REAL* MAGIC.

getting paid for it. You're on your way to making a living as a lounge singer.

For you office entertainers—*no day-care centers*, please. These places are breeding grounds of contagion. There are more germs in a day-care center than Tom Jones has fans. And they're all dying to jump on you. These are some groupies you don't need.

At home, try turning your rumpus room into the Aladdin Room. Offer dinner and cocktail shows. Practice snappy repartee. Let your children be the hecklers. The important thing is practice, practice, practice.

AGENTS, ATTORNEYS, PIT BOSSES AND OTHER SCHMUCKS

I fired him.

I finally did it.

I fired my agent.

After fifteen years, I got rid of the bastard. Fifteen years of no returned phone calls. Fifteen years of the fancy stationery with offices everywhere—Zurich, Cairo, Tokyo. Why am I carrying Tokyo? Who needs Cairo? I need Laughlin.

I got rid of the clown because I'm sick and tired of paying ten percent of my gross for nothing. Ten percent! Of everything I do! Going to this lazy, two-bit, miserable . . .

Excuse me a second.

I'm sorry. I'm back. It was my agent. He got me a gig in Laughlin.

Okay, he's back on the payroll. But one more mistake and he's gone. Vamoose.

I don't have to tell you that lawyers are the worst. Everybody knows that. They're low-down, blabbermouth, double-talking good-for-nothings who prey on this country's most valuable resource—lounge singers. They're vampires in pinstripes. They over-talk, over-lunch, and over-charge. How many times have you tried to call your attorney at Schunzio, Hunzio, and Nunzio only to be told, "He's down the hall in a meeting." How many halls are there in this place? And what's he doing meeting in a hall, anyway? He doesn't pick up the phone for less than three hundred bucks and when he does, all you hear are hereunders, heretofores, and whereases. He can kiss my whereases. I hate these guys. I've hired and fired the best in the business.

But my new attorney, Antoine, is very, very special. What sets him apart is the way he *dresses*. When he represents me, Antoine wears the very same things I wear onstage. We shop together. I've opened accounts for him at several of my favorite stores. When Antoine works for me, he *looks* like me—the spectacular jackets, the coiffed hair, the jewelry. Talking to him is just like talking to me, Bud E. Luv. Except he knows Latin.

That's the way it is. And that's the way it should be.

Pit bosses are a whole other breed of cat. They run the casino. Their job is to make sure you start and end your show on time. If you don't, you eat into the profits of the casino. The pit boss won't like that. Neither will his friends. Remember: Somebody gave that pit boss a job. And it wasn't Mother Teresa.

Years ago in Vegas, a nice kid named Donny O'Day ran five minutes over in his show. I go backstage—no Donny. I go to the limo—no limo. I go to his hotel suite— no hotel suite. Just cinders smoldering. And on the ground, the faint outline of a melted polyester tuxedo. (This was still the early seventies.)

So, invest in a good watch. Make sure it works to the second. And remember, your pit boss is on Nevada Standard Time—N.S.T.—No Singing Too-long.

A variety of other parasites come under the heading I call "Other Schmucks." These are phone solicitors, business managers, investment clowns, real estate goons, ex-wives, and deranged fans. Like that nut who shot Lennon. My advice? Lose them. Don't sign anything. Don't agree to anything. Don't say anything to these guys. Except "scram."

YIDDISH:
HOW AND WHEN TO USE IT

The Hebrew religion began in the desert. Gambling and lounge singing began in the desert. How very appropriate that they should meet in this business we call show.

Some of my very best friends are of the Hebrew persuasion. It is a great cultural tradition. On Jewish holidays, I often call them up to express warm feelings. They have a marvelous language called Yiddish. Yiddish is a combination of German, Hebrew, Czech, some Spanish, and, I believe, Navajo Indian.

You don't need to speak Yiddish fluently to be a successful lounge singer. However, you should be familiar with a few key words.

HEBE. Don't *ever* use this one. It's derogatory and it's tacky.

GISH. A movie star who's all through.

FACOCKTAH. All messed up.

SCHWARZENEGGER. A tough guy.

NOODGE. A whiner.

FENEGALAH. A dear friend.

SHEBOYGAN. The whole shootin' match, as in "the whole sheboygan."

SCHADDUP. Be quiet.

GABLE. A great pad in the Hollywood Hills, as in "such a gable."

SCHIMPL. Not complicated.

Yiddish is most effective when sprinkled in everyday conversation—like black pepper ground at the table. Use your *oy veys* and *meshuggeners* sparingly. They give people headaches. One final tip: When you're around your Jewish friends, always complain about your health. They'll appreciate it.

ST. GENESIUS, GUIDE MY CAREER

I was fortunate enough to have a private audience with His Holiness Pope John XXIII many years ago. I was eight at the time. We were at the pontiff's summer get-away, Castel Gandolfo. The camerlengo left the room for a minute, and I was admiring the jewels in the pope's hat. When it comes to fashion, ain't nobody can mess with the Supreme Pontiff.

Suddenly, His Holiness, who was a very sensitive man, a very holy man, looked into my eyes and said: *"Budulus, ego tibi do aiutum cum careerum."* I loved what he was trying to do with Latin. And he proceeded to tell me the story of St. Genesius.

St. Genesius was a lounge singer in ancient Rome who was thrown to the lions in the Circus Maximus, way before the hotel was even *planned*. He was a holy man, and a pretty good dancer. Facing almost certain death before the lions, he prayed to God and swung right into the "All Roads Lead to Rome" medley. The lions laid down like shag rugs at his feet.

I was in tears at the end of the story. Then, His Holiness, Pope John XXIII reached into his jewelry box and said, *"Budulus, ego tibi do medallionem. Buona fortuna."* And with these words, he placed a beautiful medallion around my neck. On it was the image of St. Genesius, the patron saint of show business. Since I started wearing this medallion, my prices have doubled and tripled every third year.

To this day, I return to the Vatican every Easter to do a private performance as an expression of my gratitude. I accept no fee. I do it for free. I do it for His Holiness.

MOB TIES (AND I DON'T MEAN NECKWEAR!)

I wish I had a set of brass knuckles for every person who has asked me, "Bud E., do you have to be in the Mob to make it as a lounge singer?"

Of course not.

But I'm not naive. I know there are certain people who say that, during the forties and fifties, there were certain entertainers working in certain main rooms and lounges in certain towns in Nevada who *may* have had assistance in their careers from certain individuals from a certain isle in Italy.

Okay. I know heroin doesn't wander into this country by itself. Someone accompanies it. I'm aware that when you can't get a bank loan, there are other people to see. I know protection money isn't money you spend on deodorant. I realize that some of the profits from casinos occasionally disappear before they're counted. And that some of the people involved with these activities eat spaghetti and veal sometimes. Fine.

But that doesn't mean that every lounge entertainer you see on a stage is propped up with Mob money.

I'm a friendly person. I have many friends. You understand? I make friends easily, and I don't *forget* my friends. And yes, some of my friends are of Italian extraction and noble lineage. I don't apologize for this. In fact, I frequently dedicate songs to them when they're present in the lounge—because they're friends.

Does this make me a heroin dealer? Is Bud E. Luv running numbers? Am I loaning money at usurious rates? Am I a pimp? Come on, people! Grow up! We're not watching a *Godfather* movie.

I make *music*. That's my business. I work in a casino. That's someone else's business. I make my money, they make theirs. *Buono*.

All you need to remember is this: Lounge singers don't make enemies. We're legends, but we're expendable. *Capeesh?*

Make friends, and always cook with olive oil. If there's someone in the audience whose name ends in a vowel or two, good. Be nice to them. They'll be nice to you.

Italian Words You Need to Know Besides *Volare*

Start with "Amore"—Italian for love. Look what Dino did with it. When I sing in Naples, they call me "Bud E. Amore." I like that.

ARRIVEDERCI. Another one of my favorite Italian words. It means *good-bye*. Pick up Mario Lanza's classic recording of "Arrivederci Roma" and allow yourself to be spellbound.

CONSIGLIERE. Italian for adviser or counselor. This is the man who should have your ear most of the time. Sometimes, just to be cute, I call my valet, Leon, my *consigliere*. He loves the way I say it.

PASTA FAZOOL. It's some kind of mishmash noodle and bean nightmare. But Sicilians go nuts for this stuff. Have it on hand and get used to it. And plan to hear a lot of slurping.

DICA. Italian for *speak*. This is a sign that whoever's listening wants your undying loyalty. Give it to them.

CAPO DI TUTTI CAPI. A fat guy. But don't give him any trouble. He can get grouchy with the best of them.

OMERTA. Means *shut up*.

CIAO. A friendly, international way to say *good-bye*. Sophia Loren loved it when I said it leaving her apartment in Rome.

CHIAROSCURO. Italian for light and dark. It's a word I like to use to describe certain pieces of my wardrobe. Not a word to use everywhere. It requires extraordinary sensitivity.

SENATE HEARINGS: WHAT TO SING

Many years ago, I was invited to testify in Washington, D.C., before a Senate subcommittee investigating organized crime in Nevada. They said they wanted me to sing. I never turn down a request, so I agreed. It was in all the papers.

I picked a little number I felt would work in the room. It needed to be a familiar favorite, yet fresh and, above all, lively. So I performed "Around the World in 80 Days." The chart was hot, the acoustics remarkable. It slayed them. Estes Kefauver was crying. Even the young Bobby Kennedy was nodding his tousled head and smiling.

I signed some glossies for the senators' wives, ate navy bean soup in the Senate cafeteria, and went over to the Hilton later with Bob Packwood and Everett Dirksen for a couple of pops.

I'd be in the can today if it weren't for my choice of material.

If you're called to a Senate hearing, choose your set carefully. Know what you're going to sing. Even though it's a captive audience, it's a tough room and a sophisticated crowd. Keep it lively. Sing your heart out, remember the lyrics, and remember what to forget—everything else.

Broads, Chicks, and Dolls

Is it the way I dress? Is it the way I walk? Is it the gold and diamonds dripping from my fingers? Is it the hair, each strand perfectly in place, thanks to two or perhaps three cans of professional-strength styling spray?

What are Bud E. Luv's *love* secrets?

Keep reading, my friends, and you shall see.

NOTE HOW A HANDSOME PLAID SAYS
"TOP OF THE MORNING!" BETTER THAN
ANY OTHER FABRIC.

SUSAN MUNROE

It's a well-known fact that chicks flip for the Budster. They fly off the handle. Ask my first and seventh wife, Sheila Cornucopia. It's been proven in city after city, country after country, on continent after continent. Bud E. Luv is the most. How many languages has it been said in? Too many to count.

Chicks talk, and they gossip among themselves. This cat's that, that cat's this, this cat's hot, that cat ain't. You know the bit. It's their favorite pastime, besides talking about clothes, hair, and makeup.

All right, hold it. I know what *some* of you are thinking. It's the nineties. The Women's Lib bit. And you're thinking Bud E. Luv is a male chauvinist.

Nothing, dear ladies . . . Can I say dear ladies? . . . could be further from the truth. Come spend the night at my ranch and see. Walk away from this experience if you can, and tell your friends in all honesty, that Bud E. Luv is a chauve. Legend? Yes. Legendary lover? Yes. Consummate gentleman? Yes. Chauvinist pig? I think not.

Just because a cat has all the confidence in the world doesn't mean that he's a pig. Do I look like a pig? Do I dress like a pig? Do I act like a pig? No. Then why would I ever treat a dame like a pig? I wouldn't.

You're a broad. You want me. You know it. There's nothing wrong with that, and there's nothing wrong with admitting it. There's nothing wrong with desiring me with every fiber of your being.

WHY BABES GO BONKERS
FOR THE BUDSTER

To want me is merely to be alive. To feel the rush. To feel it sweep over you like the morning tide on a beach in Maine. Your mood may be stormy. It may be peaceful. The desire may come upon you softly. Or perhaps it hits you like a bucket of water in the face. It doesn't matter how the feeling encompasses your being. All that matters is that you crave me, and that I am the most.

The first woman to tell me that I was the most was my mother, Perithea. It was during one of my olive oil baths, the special baths she reserved for holidays. It was Greek Easter. I was five. She looked into my brown eyes and said, "Bud E., you're the most."

That made it a fact. It confirmed what I suspected all along—I had it with the chicks.

At six, I was dating. By the time I was eight, I was engaged. But I broke it off—we were wrong for each other. At eleven, the girls were calling me Mr. Ed. By fourteen, I had changed my telephone number three times. Man, was I popular.

But I like to think it was more than my body. Like Marilyn, there was something tragic and vulnerable about me. Something in my look, something in my eyes that made the chicks want to be close, to learn more. I don't think I've ever lost that special appeal. But that's only my opinion.

Now, you cats are thinking, "Hey, Bud E., tell us how we can get the chicks."

Chapter Three, my friends. Dressing. Start there. Don't dress like an extra on the "Beverly Hillbillies."

Lose the Don Ameche look. It doesn't fly. I've talked myself blue in the face on this. If you want to make it with the babes, remember one word—*threads*.

HOW I SPELL ROMANCE

How do I spell *romance?* A-T-T-E-N-T-I-O-N. What does it mean? Check it out . . .

A—Attitude
T—Titillation
T—Touching
E—Emotion
N—Negligee
T—Truth
I—Intellect
O—Openness
N—Nudity

ATTITUDE. All important. Yes, it starts with the clothes, the hair, the jewelry. But it's much, much more. Confidence. A dash of arrogance. Something that's beginning to be a swagger. You know who you are. You don't know who *she* is yet, true. But the confident man learns quickly.

TITILLATION. Drive the broad nuts with innuendo. Flirt up a desert storm. Make every move, every utterance provocative. Hint that an evening with you might be more than she can handle. Close it with a sly wink. The key here is flirt, flirt, flirt. Double entendres are critical.

TOUCHING. The secret is *lightness*. Don't grab her butt and crush her with a bear hug. It's too early for that. She's still making up her mind. Run your index finger down the bridge of her nose. Touch her forearm gently, reassuringly. Take her hand and admire the lifeline in her palm. Broads love that stuff.

EMOTION. This is crucial. Don't be a stiff. Lose the Mount Rushmore vibe. Dames love passion, vulnerability. They like the feeling a cat might fly a little out of control. I'm Greek. We're emotional people. Act Greek. But don't be a statue. Gesture with your hands. Cry.

NEGLIGEE. The moment is at hand. She's at your crib. She feels vulnerable. She's not sure what to do. This is the time to give her a negligee. Something silky and sexy, but not lurid. Forget the *Hustler* stuff. Maybe something from Victoria's Secret. It'll work wonders. She emerges from your dressing area and looks breathtaking. You're in business.

TRUTH. Easy, easy. Sure you want to jump her on the waterbed. Not so fast, pal. The moment of *truth* has arrived. This is where you say something profound, something philosophical, something that will resonate with ageless meaning the rest of the evening. Down deep inside, your babe is scared, insecure. She wants to know who she's with, that it's not just superficial. Show her you have depth. Say an important truth. Try this—"Life's *more* than a pink Cadillac on the freeway of love—it's a *limousine*."

INTELLECT. Now, let her know there's something behind the rippling muscles, the bronze tan, the dancing eyes. Show her there's a bustling city of activity underneath your hair. Broads buy the complete package. Use big words. Quote a famous author. But not for long—she's getting cold.

OPENNESS. This is where you demonstrate that your heart is open to love. You're ready to receive and give emotion. Say "I'm yours" with your body language. An easygoing smile may do it. Outstretched arms are good. This makes chicks relax.

NUDITY. *Now*, you're ready. Simply remove the negligee and reveal what That Cat Upstairs has put together in His infinite wisdom. Isn't she beautiful? Isn't she lovely? Did the Budster steer you right, or what?

SENSITIVITY: MORE THAN A FEELING

Sensitivity is an intangible thing. It's not a jewel. You can't buy it. You can't buff it. It has to be there. You must cultivate it. Like an oyster. But it's not a pearl. You can't hang it on a chain. And you can't bake it like an oyster.

Sensitivity is a quality. It's an ability to understand feelings without having to be told what they are. If a dame catches you with another dame, you can *sense* she's pissed. You're sensitive. You don't have to be told. If someone's crying, you know intuitively they're upset. Again, no one has to tell you. Your sensitivity tells you.

A lot of people think sensitivity is just for broads. Don't be fooled. Sensitivity attracts dames like a magnet. Cats like Mozart, Liszt, Picasso, Warren Beatty—they have it. And oh my God, the broads! Sensitivity enables a cat to identify with chicks, to know what they're going through.

Work on having sensitive eyes. Practice looking slightly wounded. Pout occasionally. Close your eyes from time to time, as if the sight of life has suddenly become too much for you. Don't do this while walking. Burst into tears for no apparent reason.

Now, there are people who claim that it's impossible to be, or even appear, sensitive while wearing top-notch clothing. These people are charlatans. They're perpetrators—perpetrators of the myth that being sensitive means you have to look disheveled and ill-groomed. These cheapskates live in a dream world. They think chicks are going to fall for a clown in blue jeans with an out-of-tune harmonica in his mouth. Bull pucky. That's like saying one of those guys with a squeegee at the stop light is going to whisk your babe away in a Town Car. I think not.

Take Neil Diamond, for example. He does a sensitive thing. He does a brooding thing. The lips, the sleepy eyes, the hair deliberately out of place. But when the chicks show up at his suite, does he greet them wearing a torn wrapper? No. He's not Neil *Denim*. He's diamond. And cashmere, and silk, and 400-count pima cotton. And he still looks sensitive as hell, doesn't he?

SUSAN MUNROE

WHAT CAN I SAY? SHE'S STILL CRAZY
ABOUT ME AFTER ALL THESE
MARRIAGES.

So, don't buy the James-Taylor-Forever-In-Blue-Jeans crap. You know it's a lie. It's wrong. And it doesn't work. If you want your clothes to come off quickly when you're with the broads, wear clothes that are worth taking off. Don't let them fall off. Clothes are the difference between suite people and street people.

BEING AN IMPULSIVE CAT

From time to time, a perfectly sensitive individual will walk up to me and say, "Bud E., it's not working. I'm not getting laid. I'm being sensitive, and it's getting me nowhere. I cry frequently for little or no apparent reason. I admire subtleties in fabrics. I'm unhappy when bugs die. And yet I'm ignored."

I feel bad for these cats. They're trying hard. They're honest men. But they're missing an important truth about chicks: They dig *contradiction*.

Chicks eat it up when a cat does a 180. Sinatra knows it. Sammy knew it. The Beatles knew it. Trini Lopez was unsure about it. A cat whispers sweet nothings, then yells at the top of his lungs. He's Hurricane Andrew one day—and Andy Griffith the next. One minute you can't get the cat off the couch with a spatula, the next minute he's flipping you first-class tickets to Jamaica—the plane leaves in an hour. Forget the bikini!

What's happened?

He's possessed.

He's in a spell.

And the chick he's with has just turned into putty.

Why?

Because the cat is *not boring*. He's not the same schmuck day after day. He's *impulsive*. Unpredictable. Impossible to resist.

My friends, I am that Everyman. That Everywhim, that Everyluv. You should be, too.

Let me give you an example. The average clown—what does he do with a plate? He eats off it like a dog. The wife is bored to death—serving the plate, removing the plate, night after night—and fantasizing about me.

The sensitive, impulsive cat—what does he do with a plate? Better still, what *doesn't* he do with it? He dines on it. He admires its delicate Fragonard design. He removes it from the table. He washes it. Later, he has a temper tantrum and breaks it on the floor. The next day, the plate becomes a gift. He buys a replacement—a beautiful Wedgwood set, perhaps. The plate is not merely an object, it's a revolving panoply of personalities. It's kitchenware, sure. But the impulsive cat knows it's also an aphrodisiac. In the hands of a sensitive, impulsive man, a mere plate can become a dozen red roses, a love ballad, a potent weapon of romance.

Practice being impulsive at your place of employment. Walk in one day and give everyone the day off, even though you're not the boss. Park in someone else's parking space. Drive their car home. Call the phone company and have the business number changed. When your boss inquires why you've done these things, say you have no more idea than he does.

Don't be just one cat when you can be a litter. Be mercurial. Be impulsive.

But make sure the chicks see you being impulsive.

BROADS, CHICKS, AND DOLLS

When the babes at your office get wind of the fact that you're Mr. Impulsive, they'll blow into your life like a scirocco.

24-HOUR WEDDING CHAPELS: MY PERSONAL FAVORITES

Nothing says *impulsive* like a hasty wedding.

They're the best.

Low stress. Unplanned. Desperately romantic.

What a hasty wedding lacks in dignity it more than makes up for in sheer magic.

Cher did it with Greg Allman. Lola and I did it. Charo and I have threatened to do it many times. All it takes is you, a babe, and a limo.

A few years ago, at a particularly successful juncture in my career, when I was investing heavily in Las Vegas real estate, I built a 24-hour wedding chapel— The Chapel of Luv. Maybe you've heard of it. Maybe you've been there. Or maybe you know others who have been there.

Our courteous, efficient staff is always prepared to serve you—twenty-four hours a day. The Luv Boutique features jewelry and gems that I have personally selected. Credit cards are accepted, of course. The chapel seats four—ample room for you, your babe, your chauffeur, and your valet. If the chick needs a maid of honor, we have one—on video.

The Spanish Colonial chapel is spacious, yet intimate and tasteful. The stained-glass windows—illuminated by a subtle combination of daylight and neon when necessary—are peppermint pink. Music from my album, "Hits for Restless Lovers," is provided around the clock in Sensurround sound.

After the ceremony, why not relax in a bridal suite at my good friend Cy Pinella's Motel Saltimbanco. Heart-shaped waterbeds, rose-colored satin sheets, overhead mirrors, of course. And don't think of expense. Affordable chapel and motel packages can be arranged on the spot without any notice whatsoever.

When it comes to being impulsive, be prepared. For more information on our 24-hour wedding chapel, write to: Chapel of Luv, Box 711, Las Vegas, Nevada 85103. It's on me.

MARRIAGES, PALIMONY, AND PATERNITY SUITS

What God has joined together, let no man put asunder.

The vow.

The ring.

The commitment.

Let's face the organ music.

Since time immemorial, men and women have married. They have taken sacred vows, borne children, and lived together in the holy state of matrimony. That's the way it's supposed to be. And for millions of lounge singers, that's the way it is.

Marriage is good.

Look at it this way. Broads look great in bridal

THE TELETHON IS ALWAYS
A GREAT TIME TO GET
TOGETHER WITH EX-WIVES.
HERE I AM WITH MY FIFTH AND
SEVENTH WIFE, SHEILA
CORNUCOPIA.

WELCOME MDA
JERRY LEW
LABOR DAY TELET

gowns. And they know it. Does every babe in a bridal gown want her picture taken a zillion times? Yes.

Why?

Because it's the most important *dress* of her life. A symbol of pride. A sign of acceptance. Commitment.

The family's crying. Relatives are crying. Friends are crying. Everybody's crying, except the caterer. He's turning a profit, and that's good. The economy is strengthened.

Weddings. Everybody loves 'em. Mothers-in-law love 'em. Hollywood loves 'em. Movies end with them, and families begin with them. Till death do us part.

Fine. Beautiful.

But people, remember, God is an impulsive cat. That's why he created divorce.

For some people, this reality is too cold. They shy away from marriage to avoid divorce. This is like never buying a limousine so you can avoid maintenance. True, you avoid maintenance. But you're walking everywhere. How do your feet feel? You could've been in Vegas days ago, but no. You're hitchhiking on the highway in 115-degree heat—to avoid commitment.

Let's stop kidding ourselves. There's a natural pattern to all things, including the marital vows. We get married, we get divorced. As often as necessary. It's part of the natural flow.

A lounge singer is attuned to the subtleties of nature. He listens. He pays attention to the fragile biorhythms of the environment. He knows that there are natural laws that must be obeyed. He cares.

Like the Native American lounge singers before

him, he knows that the earth is his mother. And that she has her rules. Who is he to disobey?

One of her rules—*get married.*

Another one of her rules—*you may get divorced.*

The reasons are mysterious, almost mystical. We cannot know the "why" of marriage and divorce. We can only allow for it in our budgets.

Now, I know some of you are saying: "But Bud E., I don't wanna get married. I can't afford a divorce."

What are you, a penny pincher? A nobody? Whoever heard of a lounge singer who can't afford a divorce?

What, are you scared of a judge? Are you afraid of some clown in a black dress who says you owe a broad some money? Grow up.

You want a dame, you marry her. You get sick of her, you divorce her. And you pay the bill.

Frank's done it I don't know how many times. Sammy with the Swedish broad. Carson. Liz. Me. How many times? Who cares? We pay the bill; we're part of nature.

Get real, pal. Broads cost money. Get into the chapel. Get married. Get divorced. Join the human race. The earth is your mother. And you need a mother-in-law.

All right, all right. I've heard it a thousand times. "Isn't it terrible about this palimony?"

Some broad gets ten million. Another gets twenty million.

Good.

Because if you get hit with a palimony suit, you're a wimp. A wuss. A baby.

You don't want to share your bag of cookies. You

don't want to play by nature's rules. You don't want to commit.

Fine. Then let the judge commit for you. He's good with an adding machine. And you're a sucker.

If you think you're going to get off the hook because you didn't marry the broad, guess again. This is Vegas. The odds favor the house, and the house goes to the dame. You're going to end up in the *dog*house, forking it over. *Capeesh?*

Now, let's turn to the subject of paternity suits. Are they a good thing? Yes, by all means. What do you do about them? Two things:

A. Get a good attorney.
B. Get a good publicist.

You want a good attorney because you want to appear annoyed by the suit. Your attorney should snarl, act indignant, and refuse to discuss the case with the press.

You want a good publicist because you want to maximize the image enhancement that comes with a casual pregnancy. You're a stud. You and the broad got crazy, no one used protection, and of course she got pregnant. Anyone would have. Your publicist can make the most out of this. He (or she) can leak the lurid details about the affair, the generous settlement, the whole bit to the tabloids. Suddenly, you're larger than life and a little more dangerous onstage. Good news for the career. And it only cost you a coupla hundred grand.

The only mistake you can make with a paternity suit is not milking it for good publicity.

BROADS, CHICKS, AND DOLLS

BODYGUARDS

Throughout the course of American history, a very small number of lounge singers have been assassinated. There was Sam Cooke. Timmy Rissoto in Detroit. And my close friend John Lennon. But for the most part, lounge singers threaten no one. And consequently, very few people threaten lounge singers. So, naturally, the question arises: Does a lounge singer really need bodyguards?

Oddly, the answer is yes.

But not for the reasons you might think.

The successful lounge singer requires at least one bodyguard at all times—to protect his hair. Remember, you have an investment, and loft, to protect. If you're wearing a piece, your bodyguard should be packing a piece.

You may well need another bodyguard for wardrobe. The world is full of grape juice and sharp objects that can stain and tear fine fabric. Don't be naive. Someone could spill a pizza on you, soil you with a Hershey bar, or rip your wardrobe with a fork.

Personally, I also have a bodyguard for jewelry. The reasons are obvious. The jewelry is obvious.

It's also wise to have a bodyguard to protect you from photographers. You should have your own personal photographer, who can double as your bodyguard.

People ask me, "What is the proper physique for a bodyguard?" A bodyguard should look like a concrete

THE HOUND DOG MAN AND SAMMY DAVIS, JR.,
BACKSTAGE IN VEGAS. NOTICE THE BODYGUARD
PRACTICING NEEDLESS LIP EXERCISES.

YOU OUGHTA BE ME

block wall in a suit. He should look uncomfortable in his clothes, especially his necktie. If your bodyguard can buy a shirt that fits his neck, fire him. He's too small. From time to time, your bodyguard's pants should explode.

There have been successful midget bodyguards who rely chiefly on biting. I don't recommend it. Rabies shots are expensive, and you can be sued.

Where do you find bodyguards?

Football teams, obviously. Any of your Gold's Gyms. Wrecking crews. The world of professional wrestling. The world of professional *mud* wrestling.

Don't overlook the *woman* bodyguard. Broads who pump iron have a point to prove. I had a young woman bodyguard for several years. People saw the bra and laughed. I can't count the number of people she threw out the window. We're still close friends.

It's important to practice walking with your bodyguards. If you don't, they'll be on your Guccis in a minute. To avoid injury while you're practicing, wear steel-toe boots. Practice lateral formations, flanking, closing ranks. If you don't have bodyguards, practice with your children or friends.

To All the Chicks
I Loved Before Julio Did

Dear Ladies,
This is an open love letter from Bud E. Luv. This is the moment . . . can I say moment? . . . in my book

where I pause and reflect on the vast number of women who have shared their beauty, physical and spiritual, with me.

I am humbled. I am grateful. I was inspired by each and every one of you to give you all of my love. I will go to my grave remembering the passion, the tumult, the natural lubricants, and the inevitable release of our love. Those moments were as liberating for me as I know they were for you. We flew, we soared, we truly made love.

Can any man on this planet say he's been luckier than I? I think not. Life is gone in an instant. Stars explode and flicker out. Only memories and diamonds remain.

To all the girls I loved before Julio did, I honestly adore each and every one of you. You have made my stardom unique. You have blessed my life. From my mother, Perithea, to that little lass in Kansas, to the steelworker in Wilkes-Barre, to the Keno girls in Reno, Tahoe, and Laughlin, to the starlets too numerous to mention, thank you all. You have embroidered my life. You are my life.

PHOTO BY PHILLIP BISSADA

"THIS CAT TAUGHT
ME EVERYTHING I KNOW."
—JAMES BROWN

NINE

Becoming a Legend

Like a hawk, I'm floating over the mountains, soaring on the thermals of my own genius. America lies below me. I feel flushed with perspective. Is that Nevada? Yes. I can dimly make out Caesar's Palace. Far to the north, I see Wayne Newton's ranch. And beyond, the great California coast. Hollywood. Bel Air. And beyond that, the Orient.

I see the Grand Canyon, and its majesty reminds me of the impact I've had on so many careers. There's been the struggle, and the ultimate triumph. There's been pain, and marvelous victories. But most of all I cherish the supreme reward—the reward of becoming a legend.

LEGENDS I'VE CREATED

And yet, I'm haunted.

Haunted by one of my failures.

The one that got away.

I speak of the man called "The King." A man I called friend.

Elvis and I were from different states, from different parts of the world. He grew up in the country. I grew up in the city. Maybe that's part of what went wrong!

He was a man of simple tastes. Coca-Colas, Nutty Buddies, lavender Cadillacs. He was like a kid in a candy store. I loved his innocence. But it's too late now. The hound-dog man is gone.

I still wake up in the middle of the night wondering how I failed him. Did I give him the wrong moves? I told him a thousand times the cape was wrong. Should I have stopped him from singing "In the Ghetto"? I could have been tougher. He would have listened. I know it, now.

When I introduced Elvis to Ann-Margret, I thought we were on the right track. Colonel Tom was jubilant. I was thrilled. At last, Elvis would play Vegas. He would find his real calling.

The teeny-bopper scene wasn't real, and Elvis knew it. Elvis was becoming a cartoon. The endless concert tours, the screaming twelve-year-olds, the bad movies were eating away at the core of the man.

He used to say to me, "Bud E., I know it's wrong, but I can't stop it. It's bigger than I am. It's even bigger than my belt buckle." That's how big it was.

It was my hope—no, my prayer—that by returning to Vegas, Elvis would finally take his rightful place in the lounge. There he would find acceptance. Intimacy. Warmth. Drinks with umbrellas in them. Something normal. Rational people enjoying music and cocktails. He could have been himself, not the swollen, drug-riddled puppet he grew into.

Oh, sure, he played the Hilton. But he played the *main room*. He continued the madness. The lounge beckoned, then sat by, empty and crestfallen.

In 1977, he succumbed to abuse. I believe the lounge could have saved him. But no. I lost a friend, and one of my greatest protégés. I live with that loss every day, and I blame myself.

Fortunately, not every story of stardom ends in tragedy. I'm so proud of what Sammy was able to do with my material and guidance. He came to me after the accident, convinced he'd never be the same after losing one eye. I gave it to him straight: "Lose the patch. You look like a Hathaway shirt ad." I called Sandy Dennis and Peter Falk for a little support. And from then on, Sammy never looked back. He couldn't. He just knocked 'em dead the world over.

Francis Albert Sinatra. The Chairman. What can I possibly say about Sinatra? The best saloon singer on the

WAYNE NEWTON: I SUGGESTED THE IDEA OF THE MUSTACHE *NOT* MEETING IN THE MIDDLE. HE SOARED WITH IT.

planet? Definitely. And Frank takes direction beautifully. When I helped him make the adjustment from swing to bossa nova, he was so supple. His instincts were flawless. He sang my arrangements as if he'd written them himself. And the very few suggestions I made to him about his tone enabled him to soar. Every teacher should have such a student. I love Frank—and Jilly, if you're listening, I'll keep an eye on him.

So many others. Peter. Charo. Wayne. Michael. Tom. Gwen. Jack. Tony. What times we had. They all came to me at different junctures in their careers. I never said the same thing twice. Each throat, each personality, each tuxedo calls for something a little different. They've all had great triumphs.

But there's still Elvis.

THE LARGER-THAN-LIFE
PERSONALITY: A MUST

Where does a legend begin?

It begins as a tiny seed in the entertainer's own mind. He may be six, he may be three. He may be waddling around in diapers. But he believes in himself. And he already possesses a crucial ingredient: the Larger-Than-Life Personality.

People don't part with a hundred bucks to see some ordinary schmo stand around on a stage. They pay to see charisma, stature, self-assurance, style, loft, sheen, a lacquer-like brilliance that's miles deep. They pay to see jewelry.

BECOMING A LEGEND

167

They pay to see depth, savoir faire, delicate nuances of personality. They pay to hear hits—lots of them. They pay to be enchanted, seduced, conquered. They pay to see the Larger-Than-Life Personality.

How can you become larger than life?

Elevator shoes.

Everyone wears them. Check out Tom Jones. You think he's six-one? Lifts, my friend. Newman, Redford, Hoffman. They're tiny. Charo, Pia, Dolly. Midgets.

What do they do? They use the silver screen. It makes them larger. You can do this at home or at work. Rent a 70-millimeter screen and a projector. Have someone take some close-ups of your face, and project them for your family and fellow employees. You'll look huge.

Try increasing the size of your hairdo. This is an easy way to add desperately needed inches to your stature.

The Larger-Than-Life Personality never does anything halfway. Walk into your favorite bar and buy a round of drinks for everyone there. You'll seem larger immediately.

When you get angry, don't whine and whimper. Throw a full-blown temper tantrum. Break something. Fire everyone in sight, whether they work for you or not. Then, have an enormous remorse attack later. The Larger-Than-Life Personality is mercurial, unpredictable, explosive. Work on it. Change your mind about things quickly and passionately.

Practice having a prodigious appetite. Order twelve dozen oysters when you go to a restaurant. Make unreasonable demands. Fly in barbecue ribs from Kansas City. Have too many girlfriends. Buy something new, use it once, and throw it away instantly. Order an expensive new automobile, and have it completely refurbished.

Whatever you do, don't do it halfway.

THE LITTLE PEOPLE

The flashbulbs sizzle. The crowd surges forward. The fans strain for a closer look. The bodyguards close ranks. And suddenly, the limousine pulls away. Autographs have been signed, hearts have been won. The paparazzi have withdrawn. A legend has visited, and now retreats quietly into the night.

Yes, this is an everyday occurrence for me. It can be for you, too. And I'm sure that, after reading this book, it will be. But many, many people in the world do not live this way.

They are the little people.

Butcher, baker, insurance adjuster. Small-business owner, sulphur miner, housewife, piano tuner. I love them all. But they don't ride around in limos. They don't walk with the Lateral Glide. They shuffle. They don't wear warm-up suits. They have no microphone technique. They don't know a medley from a polyester hat.

But they do know talent. And they do have hopes and dreams—hopes and dreams of meeting, perchance touching, a legend. See them on the bus, their glazed eyes staring out the tinted windows at the desert scrub. They have no money. They have coupons. And yet, they'll spend their last cent to come see you, the lounge legend.

Your career depends on these people.

When dealing with your fans, or as I like to call them, "The Little People," be respectful. Be friendly. Be delighted by them; find them charming and refreshing. Your bodyguard will see to it that they don't get too close.

Insist on having your picture taken with them. Smile and joke with them. Be affable. Will they ever forget it? No. They will go to their graves claiming that you were a regular person, yet knowing that you were not one. Don't ever let them touch your hair.

Frequent cheap restaurants, preferably with ethnic owners. Have your photograph proudly displayed in the vestibule. Practice being seen. Wave to large booths of people you don't know. Greet the chef warmly. Over-tip. Send drinks to strangers. Pick up tabs for families with a grandmother in the group. Be at *one* with the little people.

When talking to the little people, make sure you use their names. And sprinkle your conversation with endearing words like *darling, sweetheart, paesan, mensch* and *bubeleh*. This will make you seem approachable. But remember: You're the legend, and they're the little people. And they like it that way.

CLOSE PERSONAL FRIENDS: THE LIST GOES ON

We're at 20,000 feet. There's lightning everywhere. My Learjet's in a dive. I turn to Tony Bennett and say: "You know, Tony, there's no one in this world I'd rather die with than you." He looks at me and says: "Whadaya need *me* for? Last night in Poughkeepsie, you died alone."

We throw our heads back and howl. Of course, the plane pulls out of the dive. And a short time later, we're closing a show together in Chicago.

Mr. Bennett's a close personal friend. We kid each other all the time. Close personal friends can do this.

What do I mean by close personal friend?

Allow me to explain. A *close* friend is someone you play golf with regularly, but with whom you never discuss personal matters. The friendship has value, but it's limited. Fred MacMurray is a good example for me. Fred's great. He shoots in the low 90s, and he never cheats.

A *personal* friend is someone you may see very rarely, but with whom you invariably discuss personal matters. Queen Elizabeth comes to mind. We don't hang out. But whenever we see each other, we get down. We talk about whatever may be on our minds.

A *close personal* friend is someone special. You see them regularly, *and* you are on intimate terms with them. Joey Bishop. Billy Graham. Fred Rogers. The sultan of Brunei. The list is endless.

People know lounge singers are sensitive. They watch you handle a lyric, they see you with the broads, and they feel they can talk to you. They seek you out. Before you know it, the rich and famous have come to be your close personal friends. Like you, they know it's lonely at the top. It's difficult to be a legend—the constant demands, the grueling schedule. They need someone who can understand—a bridge over troubled water. And so do you.

BECOMING A LEGEND

171

HIGH TEA AT THE RANCH, A TRADITION
THAT BEGAN WITH THE QUEEN'S FIRST VISIT.
HER MAJ SWINGS THE MOST.

Unfortunately, there aren't enough pages in this book to list *all* of my close personal friends. But I'd like to mention just a few, if I may. Ava. Eva. Princess Grace. Liz. JFK. Benny Goodman. Ike. Lenny Bruce—that cat killed me. Satchmo. Jane Russell—what a set! Ernie Kovacs and Steverino. Albert Schweitzer. Bucky Fuller. Dick Clark. Gloria Vanderbilt. Bill and Hillary Clinton. And so forth.

They've all been guests at my ranch. The very mention of their names brings back a torrent of memories. We've laughed, we've cried. We've exchanged Christmas cards; we've played cards until all hours of the day and night. We've loaned each other money. We've called each other names. If I had a million dollars for every memory, I could retire the national debt.

Cultivate your own set of close personal friends. No one can tell you who they should be. Only your heart knows. But make sure your list is endless.

GIVING LAVISH GIFTS

The legend is a generous figure. Sammy Davis, Jr., was known for his generosity. If you admired a ring or watch, you would find it gift-wrapped in your suite the next day. Once, I admired Sammy's customized Cadillac Seville that the folks at Gucci had put together for him. The next morning, there was one in my driveway. And the personalized license plates read SURPRIZ.

I've given away bracelets, necklaces, rings, cufflinks, pens, automobiles, precious first editions, clothing, and real estate to close friends as well as people I hardly knew. The sultan of Brunei, one of the wealthiest men in the world and a swinging cat, was up at my ranch several years ago. He admired the red cedar siding on the barn. Apparently, it was something you couldn't get in Brunei. I had it ripped off the barn instantly and flown on my Learjet to his palace. He was knocked out. The next year, he gave me a Pez dispenser covered with diamonds. The sultan is nuts about candy.

We give and we receive. Who's to say which is more enjoyable? Certainly not I, Bud E. Luv. But it goes with the Larger-Than-Life Lifestyle to give and receive on a massive scale.

Try being generous at the office. Start with a nice painting or sculpture in the lobby. Give it away to an employee who's special to you. This is a wonderful thing to do at a museum, by the way. "You like that Picasso? Take it home. It's on me."

Cars make splendid gifts. But you don't have to start with full-size or luxury models. First, try giving away Tonka Toys and build up from there. Jaguars and Corvettes are certain to please.

If you don't have any jewelry of your own to give away, give away your wife's. But don't be solicitous. Never give someone something they haven't previously admired. It'll seem like you're trying to buy friends. That's tacky.

A word of caution about lavish giving. There are certain things that, despite their cost, are not appropriate gifts. And it doesn't matter if they've been previously admired or not. Never give someone a foil hat. Catheters are wrong. And never give anyone a midget.

HATING THE PRESS

Why do we hate the press?

Simple.

To get more press.

Bad blood has existed between the press and lounge singers for many, many years. Sinatra is known for his short fuse with the press. So am I.

If you want to be a legend, cultivate a hatred of the press. Call them bums in daily conversation. Refuse to speak to them in public. Grant no interviews. Swear at them. Walk into a restaurant and break someone's camera, whether he's a press photographer or not. This will send a message.

Now you may be saying, "Bud E., I think that's taking it too far. I'm a gentle, laid-back person. I feel no hostility toward members of the press. Besides, I want them to *like* me."

Fine. Very reasonable. But the first reason for hating the press is to make you appear *pestered* by them. Everyone knows Super Celebrities are hounded by the press day and night. They have no peace. Consequently, they explode from time to time. This is what you should do. Hating the press will make you look more like a legend.

Second, one of the only things that can hurt your career is bad reviews. And let's face it, you're going to get 'em. Some clown writes that you died in the lounge and *poof!*—the candle's blown out. You're on your way back to playing bar mitzvahs. But if you call *all* members of the press bums, you defuse their greatest weapon— the pen—by belittling it.

Ignore reviews, and your public will ignore them with you.

By the way, I'd like to take this opportunity to thank Stephen Holden and Frank Rich at *The New York Times* for being in my corner from the beginning. You cats aren't bums. Come out to the ranch anytime.

USING ONLY ONE NAME

One of the sure signs your career has reached legendary status is when people refer to you by one name only. Elvis. Charo. Sammy. Dino. Frank. Liza. Bud E. That's all you have to say, and the lounge is packed. They say a picture's worth a thousand words. I say one name's worth a million seats.

A guy came to me the other day and asked me, "Do you think I can make it using one name?"

I said: "No, Lothar, you can't."

Why?

Euphony.

The name's gotta ring. It's gotta have punch. Pizzazz.

I'll give you an example. I was in my office in Vegas. This is a few years back. I'd just finished having lunch in my private dining room with Neil Diamond and Neil Armstrong. I was drinking a Bloody Mary without alcohol—a *Virgin* Mary—when this girl came in. She had dark hair—everywhere—and she was introduced to me: "Bud E., say hello to Louise Ciccone."

I looked at her, smiled, and had two thoughts: this drink's too spicy, and her *name's* gotta go.

Then it came to me.... I was drinking a *Virgin Mary* . . . why not name her after the drink? Why not call her *Madonna*?

I suggested it. She said, "What a coincidence, that's my confirmation name." I said, "Soar with it, sweetheart." And it was done, just like that.

I tossed her a little crucifix Vic Damone had given me, patted her on the ass, and sent her on her way. The rest you know.

MADONNA. CHARISMA? LET'S FACE IT—SHE'S GOT IT.

Madonna. I love what she's trying to do with the dance-oriented material. I question the smut thing, and the blond hair? Ouch! You can see her roots from Alex Haley's old penthouse.

I kid Madonna. But my point is made. One name is where it's at. It swings the most. And with one name, you can get bigger letters on the marquee.

HANDLING TERMINAL ILLNESS

There have been so many best-sellers about terminal illness. So many movies of the week. It's a very delicate subject. Everyone must die. We know that. And it never stops being a tragedy. Terminal illness is a cruel reality. But like a paternity suit, it can be a career booster.

Terminal illness can be used in many ways. Let's begin with the already dead. Liberace and Sammy come to mind. Their final days were pageants of bravery. A brief onstage chat about their courage and contribution can make everyone misty. Think of it as an audience fabric softener.

This can also work with people the audience has never heard of. *But make sure you dedicate a song to them.* Talking about someone who's dead without dedicating a song to them is like pouring wine without a glass. It's messy.

What about people who have a terminal illness but are still alive? There's one important rule: the audience must *already know* they're terminally ill. If they're in your audience, introduce them. Say something upbeat, but *don't mention their illness*. This isn't a birthday or wedding announcement, for Chrissake. You get up and tell your audience a guy's got Lou Gehrig's disease, and the air goes right out of your balloon. You'll never get 'em back.

On the other hand, if you introduce someone everyone *knows* is sick, and say something like, "May you live a thousand years," it'll give your show legs. Dedicate a song to them like Fleetwood Mac's "Don't Stop Thinkin' About Tomorrow."

Now, to the all-important question: How can *you*, the entertainer, benefit from terminal illness? A lounge singer can reap all of the rewards of public sympathy for having a terminal illness *without actually having one*. How? Here's where a good publicist is worth his (or her) weight in gold.

The key is innuendo and rumor. Lose a little weight. A routine visit to your doctor can be easily misinterpreted. Cancel an engagement for no reason. Rumors will swirl. Always insist that you've never felt better, that you're at the top of your game. Start wearing a hat when you've never worn one before. It'll make people curious. Are you having chemo?

Your publicist, of course, will deny all rumors of illness. But it's all in how he (or she) does it. A cavalier dismissal sends the message that all is well. An evasive "no comment" can imply that more lies beneath the surface.

The trick is to keep people guessing. Let's say I plant an article in the *Globe*—"Luv Is Ill." Do I sue for libel? No. I want the public to think maybe it's true. I want the murmuring to begin. This way, every one of my next performances is charged with emotion. It's a business bonanza. A shrewd publicist can keep this ball in the air for years.

Now, friends, if, God forbid, you should be unlucky enough to actually *have* a terminal disease, put this book down right now! What are you, nuts? You should be out having the time of your life! Go to Paris. Take a junket to Vegas. Go white-water rafting. Get out of the lounge! *Party*! And if you come to see me, Bud E. Luv, I'll put you in the front row and dedicate a song to you. Scout's honor.

T E N

Tax Write-offs

Let's get something straight right now. Lounge singers don't *make* money. Countries make money. The United States Mint makes money. That cat in England—the chancellor of the exchequer—makes money.

Lounge singers *take* money.

MY PAL NORM CROSBY AT THE
BUD E. LUV CELEBRITY PRO-AM
MINIATURE GOLF TOURNAMENT.

People stream into lounges and hand us their money. Our job is to take it. In my case, I'm not ashamed to say I've taken a lot of money for many, many years. And one of the questions I'm most frequently asked is: "Bud E., where do you hide it?"

Answer: Investments.

THE BUD E. LUV PRO-AM MINIATURE GOLF CLASSIC

The day: Sunday, November 7, 1979. The place: The Heritages Miniature Golf Estates in Horizon, Nevada, on the treacherous fourteenth green. The desert air, crystalline over the snow-capped mountains. The desert sands, a breathtaking white. The national television audience held its breath as the announcer whispered, "Arlene Francis has this putt to remain three under."

Everyone remembers Arlene missing that putt by a whisker just below the hole. And everyone recalls the thrilling three-way playoff between Arlene, Connie Stevens, and Brent Scowcroft. And talk about moments—who could forget Arlene's winning comeback drive on the eighteenth hole, through the little door in the windmill and over the puppy's tail on the other side?

It's just this sort of drama that has lent such an aura of excitement to my annual Bud E. Luv Pro-Am Miniature Golf Classic.

My tax accountants first suggested the idea of hosting a miniature golf classic years ago, figuring that someone of my stature could make the event instantly exclusive. We laid down the green velvet at the Heritages and never looked back. What am I talking about? First, we laid down the green *dough* to buy the joint! But it was worth it.

I think Jackie Gleason said it best when we played eighteen together in one of the preliminary rounds the second year. He said, "Bud E., this is a tough course. The velvet's impossible to read, but this is the premier mini-golf event in America. Thanks for having me."

And with that, the Great One canned a 21-footer. Awesome. I miss him.

I realize that it's premature for most of you to start your own golf classic. Certainly, most of you do not have the massive tax liabilities I have. But some day you may, and you'll thank me for writing this chapter.

First, find a corporate sponsor—an Alpo, a Budweiser, a Spam. Dinah Shore and Nabisco. Perfect. They're like peanut butter and jelly. Dinah and I kid each other about our classics all the time—whose is bigger, who gets the ratings. I love her. She's nutty.

Next, interest a major network in the event. Your CBS, your NBC, your Fox, your Home Shopping. Get 'em juiced for the pitch. And always talk celebrities. Tell them Liz will caddy and Julio Iglesias will do color. They'll love that. Tell them anything. Just get 'em on board.

Now, select a location. Make sure it's near a major jetport and a great hotel, preferably with a spa. Design a great logo, and plaster it everywhere—hats, shirts, pants, automobiles, and bedspreads.

Make sure your miniature golf course has a distinctive appearance. My close friend Salvador Dali put his unique stamp on the Heritages course. The melting clock on the fifth hole is unforgettable. And I'm particularly proud of *Guernica*—the tenth hole—and Salvador's personal tribute to Pablo Picasso. Nicklaus flipped for it.

The amount of money you can hide hosting an event like this every year is staggering. I write off everything associated with it. You should, too. See you there!

HOSPITAL WINGS AND PLAYGROUNDS: FAVORITE CHARITIES

I take charitable giving very seriously. I don't part with an excess of five million dollars annually without getting something for it. I want to see that money in bricks and mortar, glass and steel. And I want to see happy faces.

How do I do it? I build two things: hospital wings and playgrounds. The Bud E. Luv Vegas Throat Infirmaries—now in seven cities throughout the world—stand as a monument to my commitment to better health. We've assembled the finest team of throat research specialists on the face of the globe. Not only can we cure Vegas Throat, but we're also making startling new breakthroughs in *creating* Vegas Throat for those who need it. The equipment is first-rate. Our Lounge Simulators produce the most authentic smoke-filled air possible. When President Clinton gets a rasp, who's he gonna call? The Budster. Plus, I always know in case I have throat trouble, there's a hospital I can go to that I *own*.

Now, to playgrounds. A number of years ago, I wrote a little song for a nice kid, Clint Holmes. It was

REHEARSING FOR ONE OF THE MANY TELETHONS I DO EACH YEAR. NOTE HOW THE COFFEE CUP SUGGESTS INFORMALITY AND CONFIDENCE.

called "Playground in My Mind." He soared with it— sold a couple million copies. One day, as I hummed the lyric ... "My name is Michael, I've got a nickel"—you know the rest—I thought to myself, "We don't need playgrounds in people's minds. We need them in schoolyards." And I never looked back.

YOU OUGHTA BE ME

I called up my accountant, Arthur Traub, and immediately had him transfer some funds to our building account. The next day, we broke ground in Harlem. Then Chicago, Detroit, St. Louis, and Ogden, Utah. Rome, London, Calcutta, and Portofino were next.

I derive no monetary profit from my playgrounds. But I do get the immense satisfaction of knowing that on those jungle gyms, merry-go-rounds, and seesaws, children are smiling every day, everywhere in the world. I didn't have a playground when I was growing up. We had the street. We played football with an old carburetor. I don't want kids growing up like that today. And thanks to the Bud E. Luv International Playground Foundation, they don't have to.

GET A TELETHON!

I have always revered Mr. Jerry Lewis. I can think of no one in the entire panoply of stars I have known who has shown greater dedication to his craft and to the high-minded principles of the motion picture industry. From his days with Dean Martin in picture after picture straight through to *The King of Comedy* and *Mr. Saturday Night*, the man has owned the silver screen. A fine singer in his own right, Mr. Lewis generously stepped aside and allowed his son to bask in the musical limelight with his rock combo Gary Lewis & The Playboys. I think I wrote several of their hits.

The French worship Lewis, and I know why. His uncanny sense of comic timing, and his hair, rival those of the great Chaplin. And so it is with great pride, and humility, that I recall the day when Jerry's mother, Mrs. Lewis, came to me many, many years ago for a chat.

She said, "Bud E., I'm worried about Jerry. He's floundering spiritually. He's one of Hollywood's richest men, and yet something's wrong. He's unhappy somehow."

It was then that I had the idea for the televised charity event. I knew Jerry had the energy, the stamina. He just needed a focus. He needed a goal above and beyond the public acclaim and monetary rewards. He needed kids.

Jerry's kids.

Did he soar with it? No. For the first time in these pages, the word is inadequate. He *owns* the televised charity milieu. He's the master. No one will ever replace Jerry.

Every year, Mrs. Lewis sends me a box of Godiva chocolates with a handwritten note of thanks. But in truth, we're all in *her* debt forever. She gave birth to Mr. Jerry Lewis—the King of Comedy and the King of Charity.

Jerry, I salute you.

And speaking of salutes, I want to thank Glen Campbell for giving me the inspiration for a telethon I, Bud E. Luv, will be hosting each year beginning in 1995. It's the Annual Bud E. Luv Telethon for the Fashion Impaired.

So many unfortunate people among us suffer from fashion impairment. This crippling disease—the inability to know what to wear and when to wear it—strikes millions of people each year, leaving them trapped in garish outfits and ghoulish off-the-rack costumes. This nightmare can be averted. With counseling, audiovisual aids, and carefully monitored credit-card therapy, fashion victims can come back.

One of the cornerstones of our rehabilitation program is the very book you hold in your hand. But how can we possibly provide this book to all the millions who so desperately need it? That's where your donations come in, to fund Operation Luv Outreach.

In twenty-six consecutive hours on the air, the Annual Bud E. Luv Telethon for the Fashion Impaired will raise millions of dollars to purchase my book and distribute it to the neediest. Volunteers will man (and woman) the phones; pledges will pour in. Together, we can stop this fashion crippler.

See you on the air. And thank you for watching.

MAINTAINING THE FLEET: LEARS, LIMOS, AND STALLIONS

You're a lounge singer, right? You arrive at the stage door for one of your exclusive engagements. What do you step out of? A Nash Rambler? A Gremlin?

No.

You step out of a gleaming, full-length limousine in a color of your own choosing.

You're with a babe. At a tasteful little Italian eatery. You're having the lamb chops. She's having the special. You're feeling impulsive. Instead of ordering a cappuccino, you decide to go somewhere tropical. What are you

TAX WRITE-OFFS

PROPER LIMO
ENTRANCE.

going to take, a Piper Cub? Are you going to fly with a bunch of tank tops on a wide-bodied nightmare? No. You slip away in your very own Learjet.

It's Sunday morning at your ranch in Big Sur. You're tripping down the cobblestones. You're lookin' for fun. You're feelin' groovy. Are you on a *Schwinn*? Of course not. You and your babe are riding a pair of perfectly matched Arabian stallions. The wind is dancing playfully in her hair. You feel carefree.

Did I say carefree?

Yes. I said carefree, because you have a Maintenance Staff.

A lounge singer has an image to protect, a reputation to uphold, and a fleet of toys that bespeak success. He doesn't leave them in the hands of any clown with a sponge. He has a crack team of sanitation experts, mechanical engineers, and visionary trouble-shooters.

We don't curry our stallions ourselves. We have people to do that. We have trainers, feeders, round-the-clock veterinarians. We care for our toys the same way we care for our close personal friends. My horses have bridles, blankets, and monogrammed nosebags designed by Giorgio Armani.

When it comes to jet, automobile, and animal maintenance, plan to spend. Hire people with the right credentials, and pay them well. Check up on them from time to time. And if they don't keep your toys in top-notch condition, fire them promptly.

TAX WRITE-OFFS

191

Remember, your Learjet and limousine can be rented out to others at punishing rates to help defray the expense. People who can afford Learjets seldom look at the bills. Pad them generously.

I do not recommend yachting or the ownership of power boats. The ocean will swallow your investment whole and make your accountant seasick. I'll never forget the time John Davidson and I decided to get away from the rat race on his 96-foot Sequoia Class motor yacht, the *Principia*.

We were on our way to the South Seas with nothing more than canned food, oil paints, and dreams of reliving the final days of the great French post-Impressionist painter, Gauguin. Forty miles outside of Marina Del Rey, our compass broke. We ended up in Hudson's Bay, surrounded by icebergs and penguins. Neither of us had a tuxedo. We stood out like sore thumbs. It was freezing. And had it not been for the kindness of the Inuit people, several of whom recognized me from Merv's place in Atlantic City, we would have perished.

PURCHASING THE RIGHT RANCH

The lounge singer lives in a pressure cooker. He's at the beck and call of his public at all times, constantly dealing with the stress of being a celebrity. From time to time, he needs to kick back. That's why we purchase ranches.

Famous people love to get away to ranches. It's an American institution. I remember fondly the days I spent with my main cat, Ronnie Reagan, at the Western White House near Santa Barbara. Nancy standing in the kitchen cooking up a stack of flapjacks. The president splitting wood with Ed Meese. The cats in the Secret Service jamming on Jew's harp and washtub bass. The aroma of sagebrush. There was such an air of relaxation there.

When purchasing a ranch, the key is acreage. Never buy a ¾-acre ranch. Look for wide open spaces. There should be plenty of room to discover oil. Listen for the cry of the coyote, the hooting of the owl. Build an enormous patio and barbecue pit. And keep a case of tequila on hand—with the worm. John Wayne always loved my grill. May I recommend mesquite charcoal—ideal for fish and chicken. And remember: Never cook in your stage clothes unless you want to smell like you're headlining at Oscar's Open Pit Barbecue.

OWING THE IRS: A CAREER MOVE

The Internal Revenue Service is a fact of life. Every American citizen knows this. As lounge singers, we're not expected to like it. But taxes are not going away, and when it comes to muscle, Uncle Sam's the cat with the most. So I'd like to tackle this issue head-on.

My close friend Willie Nelson is a case in point. Since Willie and I were good old boys, doing shows together in Lubbock, Texas, Willie's always had a hankering for the good life. Sure, there's the bandanna thing, the old blue jeans, the pawnshop guitar look. I, for one, happen to like what he's been trying to do with that.

TAX WRITE-OFFS

But underneath the rags, there's a different Willie—the Willie I know. The Dom Pérignon Willie. The Cartier and Perrier Willie. High-priced spreads, lavish gifts, the whole megillah. It's all part of the Big Ticket Willie the feds walked in on.

Don't get me wrong. I feel bad for Mr. Nelson. I'm sure he received poor financial counseling. He was a victim of the free lunch syndrome: the bogus shelters, the too-good-to-be-true investments. And they all came home to roost like an ugly buzzard on a telegraph wire.

It's an American tragedy.

Or is it?

Look what happened. Willie took a bum steer by the horns. He listened to my advice. He turned his adversity into a triumph by recording and releasing a special album called *The IRS Tapes*. He straightforwardly told the public how much he owed, and begged them for their help in record sales. His fans loved it. *Presto*. Willie's out of the woods.

Owing the IRS doesn't have to be the end of it all. It can be a career move. In this sense, it is not unlike the paternity suit or terminal illness ploy. The public is automatically sympathetic to the lounge singer's quandary. They rally around him. They want to help. They want to give at the box office. And remember, your job is to *take* their offerings.

Is it right to manufacture a tax problem for public sympathy?

Yes and no.

If your career's running out of gas, the threat of having some of your assets seized by the IRS can bring you much-needed publicity. Look beleaguered. Be the underdog. Wear out-of-date clothing. But remember: A tax crisis should be used only *once* in a career. Don't go crying wolf every four years. You'll look like a deadbeat.

Fortunately, I have never had serious tax problems. But my heart goes out to my colleagues who have. Sammy, Wayne, Redd Foxx—they all got behind the eight ball. In Redd's case, I loaned him the money to get back out. In Wayne's case, I've made what I consider to be a very generous standing offer to purchase his entire. stable of Arabian horses, nosebags and all. Perhaps someday he'll take me up on it.

But don't be a chump. Pay your taxes. If the only career-stretcher you can think of is bankruptcy, you don't belong in the lounge. You belong in the savings and loan industry.

Developing an Alcohol or Drug Problem

By this point in the book, you know a lot about me. You know I'm talented; you know I love and respect broads; you know I have style; you know I have class.

But you're probably wondering, "Bud E., are you pro-choice?"

I don't blame you. I'm asked this question all the time. Famous people are always asked this question. And I'm not afraid to answer.

Let me give you the answer I gave on the Carson show—unequivocally *yes*.

I am pro-choice.

In all things. For all people.

If a woman chooses to have breast augmentation, I don't have a problem with that. It's her body. It's her decision.

If a man wants an eye tuck, it's his face. It's his call.

If you want to drink and take drugs, it's a personal choice. No one can stop you. It's your decision. I believe strongly that when it comes to clothing, jewelry, abortion, hair, musical material, cosmetic surgery, drugs, alcohol, tobacco, and firearms, *personal choice reigns.*

Allow me to say a little more, if I may, on the very delicate subject of drugs and alcohol. It's no secret that drugs and alcohol have been part of the entertainment industry since its inception. There have been tragedies; there have been victories.

Some of the world's greatest entertainers have been brutal alcoholics. They've soared with it. Others have been renowned teetotalers. And they've soared with that. Personally, I drink in moderation.

I believe in the old adage: "One man's meat is another man's poison." If you can drink a quart of Jack Daniels and still do two shows a night, more power to you. If you can shoot heroin before the show and still do the dance numbers, by all means go for it. You know the consequences.

If you want to *quit* drinking or doing drugs, fine.

But what's with all these 12-step programs?

I remember when the only 12-step program in town was Arthur Murray's. What's the first step? The samba? If one more person tells me they're in a 12-step program, I'm gonna scream!

What's the matter with you babies?

Can't you stop drinking by yourselves?

You wanna quit booze? Simple. Stop *pouring*. How many people does it take? Do you really need a room full of two hundred people drinking coffee and smoking cigarettes to help you? Wise up, people. Or take 12 steps off a short pier!

I'm sorry.

I got carried away. It's only because I care so very much.

Is "Just Say No" Just for Kids?

When Nancy Reagan came to me with the "Just Say No" idea, I said no at first. Then, I paused and reflected. I realized "Just Say No" wasn't just for kids. It's for everyone. If someone tries to give you a velvet painting for Christmas, just say no. When someone in the audience requests "Proud Mary," just say no. If anybody ever gives you polyester, just say it. No. Nancy flew with the concept, and I'm glad I could be there for her.

The magic of Garland. Nothing compares to it. Nothing. I remember doing a show with her at the Adrian Milletts Center in Queensland, Australia. The schedule was grueling. We had done three nights in the outback, and Judy was exhausted. When she went on the stage, she was completely plowed. The manager threatened to cancel the engagement. Garland wouldn't hear of it. She went onstage and punched 'em out like a kangaroo. The control, the uncanny timing, the gossamer phrasing were all there—with the urgent emotion. She weighed ninety pounds even with four martini olives in her. But every ounce of her was a fighter.

What gave her the stamina? Some say drugs, amphetamines. I question that. That's not to say that she wasn't a walking drugstore. After all, who's kidding who here? But I think it was the natural vibrancy, the tingling dynamism, the desperation of Garland that drove her. Throwing herself at her audience, night after night, basking in the adulation. I really think it was the fans who gave her the energy and the will to go on. I mean, we're talking about a walking alcohol factory here. I loved her. I know you did, too. Miss her? It's more than that. I feel the loss like a nor'easter blowing through my soul.

I should say a word here about the chicken and the egg thing. Make no mistake—with Garland, the talent came first, the booze and pills later. Her talent wasn't courtesy of Seagrams. It was in spite of it. So many young kids who open for me come into the dressing room with a quart and a half of vodka, hoping to match the intensity of Garland's performances. I think they may be deluding themselves. Yes, the choice is theirs. But the *ice* is mine. Get away from the bar! You can't drink yourself over the rainbow.

The Judy Garland legacy is not a legacy of drugs and alcohol. It's a legacy of dedication to the performing arts. Judy's career can't be measured in highballs. There was always the talent. Gargantuan. That was her true legacy. I'm still in awe, and I miss her very much.

Joe Cocker: What Good Is He Sober?

I'm so frequently asked the question "What good is Joe Cocker sober?"

I think it's a fascinating question. Embodied within it is the larger question "What happened to the good ol' days?" I think what people are doing here is confusing show business with nostalgia. They're saying that Joe was better bombed. But I suspect what they really mean is that the *times* were better, the *era* was better.

The late sixties. Platform shoes. The counterculture. Soaring freedom. People felt good. Joe *really* felt good. But was he better then? Let's look more closely.

In the early days of the Mad Dogs thing—and, by the way, I was quite opposed to the tour originally—Joe had something. A raw force. His medleys were crude. His dedications were nonexistent. He dressed like an organic farmer. But, yes, there was something there.

Now, let's cut like a shot to the present. The Greek Theater. Los Angeles. The nineties. I've just done four days there. I've got one day off before I return to Vegas. Some friends invite me to go see Joe at the Greek. For old times' sake.

He's fortysomething—cum laude. No rug. And he's sober. The band is cooking—keeping the mediums bright, swinging the ups, soulfully driving the ballads. All's well. Joe's singing—or is it yelling in pitch?—whatever. The older broads in the crowd are grooving. Some things haven't changed. Joe still can't hold a note with a pair of pliers. But who cares? The background singers are carrying him. And once again, twenty years later, he's got something. And he's *sober*.

Which is better? Which cooks the most? Which is the *real* Joe Cocker? Who's to say?

Joe, I salute your personal choice. You are so beautiful—to me.

DINO AND HIS BOOZE: THE PERFECT MARRIAGE

Dean Martin is an old, old friend. He's of Italian-American origin, and has the rugged good looks that Hollywood has always demanded of its leading men. He's been a success at everything he's put his comb through.

"When the moon hits your eye like a big pizza pie, that's a-more-aayyy."

The famous slur, the internationally known stagger, and the crowd eats it up night after night. How does Dino do it?

Juice.

No lounge-singing guide would be complete without mentioning the enormous contribution of Dean Martin, as well as that of his friends. We were always informally called the Rat Pack—Joey Bishop, Dean, Sammy, Frank, Peter Lawford, and myself. In the early days of Vegas we made history, performing in the lounges by night and prowling the casinos and suites by the dawn's early light. Those were innocent times. Jack and Bobby hadn't even started hitting on Monroe yet. America was young; Vegas was fresh.

Bishop used to crack Sammy up with a bit called Rumblefish, where he'd invite Frank or Dean over, entertain them lavishly with champagne and broads, and have his Filipino houseboy fill the trunk of their limousine with carp. When Sinatra figured out what was going on, he had Joey's swimming pool filled with dead shrimp. Frank loved chess, and he used to say he took Bishop with his prawn.

Dino and I used to finish up our shows and head out to Momo Vizzola's 24-hour skeet-shooting range. Dino was always tanked, and he never hit a pigeon. But I racked up quite a string with my 12-gauge shotgun, a personal gift from Claudine Longet. One night when Dino was particularly in the bag, he opened fire on an armored personnel carrier on desert maneuvers. Somebody got Kennedy out of bed at three in the morning. He went nuts. He called Sinatra and chewed him out for half an hour.

Great times. Great friends.

Dino's secret is the marriage—the marriage between him and the booze. They flirted, they went steady, they took the plunge. Dino never allowed the concept of sobriety to get in the way of entertaining. His wife was the bottle, and he took her everywhere. They had an onstage patter that rivaled Burns and Allen. Never desperate, unlike Garland, Dino mastered the casual "Oops, I dropped my cufflink" stage persona. When it comes to an 80-proof show, Dino swings the most. He's always good to the last drop.

Remember: Don't try to become a Dean Martin overnight. Drinking takes practice. If you start out too bombed, you'll just get arrested. You want to be in a lounge, not a lineup. Start in karaoke bars. Build gradually. On Monday night, try singing after one drink. On Tuesday, after two drinks. On Wednesday, after three. And so forth. By the third week, you should be on your way.

Dino, thanks for being the smoothest.

Ciao.

LOUNGE LIZARD TO LIZARD KING: JIM MORRISON WAS MY FRIEND

The sixties linger in my memory with a special clarity, a special feeling. And I'll never forget the day in 1967 when a good-looking young man came to my bungalow at the Beverly Hills Hotel. I was resting up from a tour of Japan with The Osmonds. The young man wore a crew cut, gray flannels, and Florsheims with rubber soles. He looked like a cadet from West Point. He introduced himself:

"Mr. Luv, my name is James Morrison. I'm in a rock 'n' roll combo named The Entrances. Somehow the rock thing isn't working for me. I want to be more like you."

There was something stiff about him, something too uptight. He needed loosening up. Yet I looked at this kid, and I had a vision. I renamed him Jim to give the act a more informal feel. We ripped open the shirt, messed up the hair, gave him the drug problem. Then we renamed the fellas The Doors, and I wrote a little lounge standard for them called "Light My Fire."

They soared with it, and Jim drove the chicks crazy. The emaciated body. The live iguana in his pants. It was all working seamlessly. Jim and I grew quite close, and I was sorry to see him headed for such a quick burnout. He could have been a permanent name on the Vegas marquees.

Towards the end, Jim moved to France, and I went to visit him in his garret in the Big Croissant. I'll never forget what he said, as he stared out the window at Montmartre, needles sticking out of his arms everywhere: "You know, Bud E., we're all just riders on the storm." It was the last song we ever wrote together. I don't miss him that much.

BETTY FORD: THE CHICK, THE CLINIC

The time was Watergate. The nation was in a state of alarm. The presidency was in a shambles.

It was such a shame.

We'd been having a blast at the White House. Particularly Sammy. Half the time, Nixon didn't even know we were there. He was asleep, or bowling. And he couldn't stand Peter Lawford.

Anyway, the next thing we know, Frank gets a call—Nixon's vamoose. Something about break-ins, missing tapes, whatever. So, we go to meet the new guy. Gerald Ford. He trips as he's coming into the room. Bishop turns to me and says, "Bud E., this guy's a stiff." The tie was too wide, the sideburns were trying too hard. It looked like the party was over.

Then we met Betty.

She sparkled, she laughed, she had a few pops. She loved Sammy. And the Pack was back. At 1600 Pennsy. Sinatra was in heaven. One weekend it was Camp David. The next it was Palm Springs. And of course, we all went to Vail in the winter. Skiing with Sammy was the best. Betty bought him a fur-lined parka.

In '76, Jerry got boomed. And we were back on the outs until Ronnie got in. But we kept up our ties with Betty. She and Jerry came up to my ranch a number of times. She was a first-rate equestrienne. She used to love to climb on one of my stallions, and ride in circles yelling "It's a roundup, it's a roundup." Jerry was expert on the barbecue. His specialty was hot dogs. All beef. Those were good times.

Years later, I was surprised, along with the rest of the nation, to learn of Betty's dependency problems. And I couldn't have been more pleased when she started her clinic at the Eisenhower Medical Center in Palm Springs, a stone's throw from Bob Hope's crib. I thought it was a great idea. A loving, caring place for celebrities to sober up. Bravo.

For years, Palm Springs had swung the most. Now, it would become America's swinging center for recovery. With Betty at the helm, the clinic would have to be a gas. She's a blast. And her courage has helped so many people stand on their own two feet again without falling over. Today, the register at the Betty Ford Clinic reads like the stars on Hollywood Boulevard. Who *hasn't* been there? I know people who've checked themselves in and don't even have a problem. Just to get the vitamins and groove with Betty.

Betty, here's a toast to you—of ginger ale. Call me whenever you need a benefit.

BEVERAGE CHOICES
OF THE STARS

In nearly three decades as a purveyor of hospitality at my ranches, at my homes, and in my limos and suites, I've served a vast assortment of beverages to a galaxy of entertainment notables. My personal bartender, Maximillian, is renowned. He stirs, blends, and swings the most. He never bruises the gin when he makes a martini. His margarita froth is the airiest. To Max, "on the rocks" means just that—he actually serves single malt scotch over frozen volcanic pebbles, adding a subtle bouquet of pumice to the cocktail. His blended libations are the smoothest anywhere in the desert.

With Max's help, I've assembled a list of the favorite beverages of some of my close personal friends. You and your guests may enjoy them as well. Remember to always use top-quality ingredients. A cheap booze hangover is an ugly guest.

CHARO. Always has a piña colada with two umbrellas in it. And she stops after ten umbrellas.

LIZA. Water.

DINO. Scotch, bourbon, vodka, gin, wine, schnapps, cognac, ale, champagne. No mixer. Real lime juice only. Hold the cherry.

JIM NABORS. Chee-chee.

TOM JONES. Dark ale. Prefers Bass.

KENNY ROGERS. Raw Oysters: Ginseng tea blended with essence of oyster and a splash of Southern Comfort.

SIEGFRIED & ROY. Shirley Temples. Two cherries. Two straws. One glass.

MR. SINATRA. Glenlivet over two cubes of ice. (Max served it over the volcanic pebbles once, and Frank punched his lights out.)

DOLLY PARTON. A Gibson Girl, in a short glass with high heels.

BETTY FORD, PAT NIXON, KITTY DUKAKIS. Water.

EDWARD G. ROBINSON. Mimosas made with fresh-squeezed orange juice and Dom Pérignon. Also, Culebras—rum with crème de cacao trapped in a serpent-shaped straw. After two, he used to put the straws under his upper lip and do a walrus impression. I miss him.

ADAM ANT. Scorpions.

SUPER AGENT SWIFTY LAZAR. Newport News—gin and raspberry juice. But he only drinks 10 percent of it.

LIZ TAYLOR. In between husbands: Dom Pérignon with a valium back. Married: water.

STEVIE NICKS. Southern Comfort, straight from the bottle.

MERV GRIFFIN. Rum and Coke Classic, tall glass.

JACK JONES. Grandma's Helper: confectioner's sugar and bourbon.

RAYMOND BURR. Maalox.

DON ADAMS, DON RICKLES, DON JOHNSON, AND DON AMECHE. Scotch.

MARLON BRANDO. Purple Cow, with a stick of butter whipped in.

WAYNE NEWTON. Water.

MIA FARROW. A Rosemary's Baby: bourbon and Prozac, straight up.

CONNIE CHUNG. Ginseng Cooler: Ginseng tea over ice, a breath of mint, and four shots of tequila.

MARLENE DIETRICH. Old Berlin: Goldwasser and Woodpecker cider.

DEVELOPING AN ALCOHOL OR DRUG PROBLEM

LUCILLE BALL. Warm gin in a coffee mug. Hold the coffee.

ROY CLARK. Cactus Cooler.

Retirement

The hair is grayer. The gait less assured. The voice is more uncertain, paler now. The energy more difficult to summon. The drugs, still easy to get, are no longer strong enough.

The time has come.

The torch must be passed.

No entertainer's career lasts forever. Ask Don Ho. The ravages of age and years of toil eventually take their toll. The entertainer must move on—step out of the limelight, into the wings.

The public will refuse to accept it at first. Your leaving makes them feel old and abandoned. It's not unlike being widowed.

Still, the time has come—the time to face the final curtain.

How to Quit:
A Tribute to Ol' Blue Eyes

Frank Sinatra came to me in the seventies with a torn heart and torn piece of paper with one word written on it—*retirement*. I looked at him and said, "Your penmanship is terrible."

I waited for the familiar chuckle.

Frank said nothing. He avoided my gaze and stared blankly at the ground.

I said, "You're kidding."

Suddenly, I realized he was serious. He wasn't kidding. The great Sinatra was calling it quits. He had five years of engagements booked around the world, and he was throwing in the towel.

I put my arm around him, and walked him into the Rose Garden. I said, "Frank, I want to paint a picture for you. It's two years from now. You're at home in Palm Springs. The phone hasn't rung for days. You wake up in the morning—there's nothing to do. You reach for the paper—there's nothing in it. *You're* not in it. You reach for your toupee—you're not in that either. There's no reason to put it on. There's no reason to get into your lifts. Your tuxedo is a useless relic. It's covered with dust.

"And that's the good news.

"The bad news is: you've been replaced. There are new names on the marquees, new bums in the lounge. They're nobodies, of course. And they're singing *your* songs. But that doesn't change anything. They're still there, like mosquito bites. And you're through. You're a has-been. Think about it. Who's going to pay for Barbara's clothes?"

We stopped.

Frank looked up at me. Then, he looked down and, without warning, crushed a centipede with his hand-sewn Italian loafers. He said nothing. He just slapped me on the back and walked away with a surprising new determination.

Frank did quit. Remember?

But guess what.

He came back.

And he planned his comeback the very same day he planned his retirement. That day with me, in the Rose Garden.

Frank Sinatra, ever the master of drama, orchestrated his *faux*-retirement with the same delicate touch he lends to his musical phrasing. How inspired. How like him.

The Chairman's retirement and return should serve as an example to all lounge singers.

Announcing Your Retirement

Does the lounge singer ever really retire?

Of course not.

Like George Burns before us, we sing right into the coffin and die with our pinkie rings on.

This is our calling.

The pope doesn't retire. He never abandons his flock. The Supreme Pontiff has a responsibility to the praying hordes. *You* have a responsibility to the paying hordes. Don't abuse it. From Vatican City to Vegas, there are no quitters.

Now, to the announcement.

The time to announce your retirement is a good fifteen to twenty years before anyone would ever expect you to quit. Don't leak the story through your press agent. Call a news conference and address the press directly. Be sincere and low-key, and plan on fighting back tears.

It's always good to use your family as a reason for retiring. Say that you want to spend more time with your children. It doesn't matter that they're in their forties. It doesn't matter if you don't have any. People love to hear this.

Another reason for retiring is to do what my close friend Ronnie Reagan did: change careers. But frankly, I have a problem with this. Oh sure, he did well with the political thing. Nancy was very happy in the White House. But when Ronnie left show business, I lost respect for him. And I think he lost respect for himself. Sure, he *looked* happy. But every time I saw him in the White House, all he talked about was the thrill of hosting "Death Valley Days."

Reagan wasn't happy. He fell victim to the grass-is-greener syndrome. You won't be happy either if you leave the lounge. There's no business like show business. Don't forget it. And don't use the old "I need a change" excuse. Your public won't buy it.

Make sure when you say you're quitting that you're at the peak, the pinnacle, the apex of your career. Don't leave the stage with your tail between your legs. Pick your moment, and stride gracefully from the top of the mountain.

I announced my retirement about ten years ago, after a long, richly rewarding career that took me to all the heights this business has to offer. I was at the top of my game. I had just created the disco phenomenon and, quite honestly, I was sick of it. I was writing disco hits for everyone, day in and day out. The capper was when Ethel Merman asked me for one. Enough was enough. I wrote a little thing called "Disco Inferno" for the Trammps, set my own 24-track studio on fire, and walked.

I told the press then that I'd had it, that show business had gone to the dogs. I also mentioned that I wanted to devote myself to adopting and caring for helpless children. I announced plans for the Bud E. Luv Home For Little Lounge Singers, and withdrew to my ranch.

Finally, I had time to myself. I went for long walks. I stared at caterpillars. I listened to the warm.

By the time six months had passed, I had cooled off.

RETIREMENT

215

One day, on one of my walks, I found myself standing in the big lounge at the Sands Hotel. It was deserted. There was a work light on, and a single microphone stood solemnly at the center of the stage. I must have stared at it for an hour and a half. The microphone began to whisper to me:

"Bud E., Bud E."

The words to my medleys began to tiptoe back into my mind. I hadn't thought of them in months. I stepped onstage and stared out at the empty seats. My life was full. My Home For Little Lounge Singers was full. And yet, I felt a void.

Suddenly, my leg trembled. I felt a surge of adrenaline. The old moves were still there. I knew I still had it. I knew I was coming back.

Was my retirement announcement more convincing because I truly believed I was through? I'll never know. But I do know there was nothing like the thrill of that first comeback concert.

PREPARING YOUR COMEBACK

If you've walked *from* the summit, as I did, you'll return to the summit. When you're ready to come back, pick a great slogan. Use the best part of your body. You don't say, "Ol' Plughead Is Back." You say, "Ol' Blue Eyes Is Back."

But don't get carried away using body parts either. And don't get too cute. You're not going anywhere with "The Return of Mr. Buttocks."

Dignity, people. Class. This is the lounge.

Okay, your public has been primed. America can feel the rush and hear the buzz. Tickets are selling like hotcakes. What do you do?

Get new clothes.

You must reinvent your look. Remember, you're coming out of retirement, not a retirement hotel. Lose the windbreaker, tennis shoes, and polyester slacks. And pull your socks up!

Set a new tone. Launch a new phase of your career with a new fashion statement. Try something youthful and fresh. Perhaps an earring. A hand-painted tuxedo. An embroidered baseball cap. A tie with cellular phones on it.

Hire new cats for your band. Find the grooviest, up-to-date hipsters who grew up with your music, love and respect it, yet swing with a little modern taste. This will bring young broads into the audience, and young broads get everyone into the lounge.

Buy new music stands for the band. Design a new logo—something familiar, yet very up to date. On opening night, give backstage passes to trendy rockers. Book yourself on all the talk shows. Publish a book, perhaps not unlike this one. Grant interviews to trendy music publications and youth-oriented magazines. Schmooze all the foreign correspondents, especially those who can't speak English. On the continent, being misquoted is sexy, a status symbol.

When asked *why* you're coming out of retirement, say you have plenty of money. It's not about the money. Say it's about something else—personal challenges—then leave the sentence hanging. This will suggest something mystical, something like a resurrection.

RETIREMENT

217

Whatever you do, always deny that you're in debt, especially to the Mob.

Wrinkles, Rugs, and Liposuction: The New You

All right, all right, all right. Hold the phone.

You're going to go onstage looking like *that*? Get a grip, pal. And then get a *mirror*.

Look at yourself.

Your face looks like a hundred miles of bad country road.

Your hair—what's left of it—has freezer burn.

You can't see your shoes without a catalogue.

Your ass is the size of the national debt. And it's growing just as fast.

Sound good? Sound like star time to you? Let me take a wild guess—you're not dating Claudia Schiffer. But you are dating yourself. Carbon 14 dating, that is.

People, turn up your hearing aids. It's Bud E. calling. And it's time for a trade-in, time for a new you. There're 150,000 miles on the old one, and you need to get to a dealer. Pronto.

The advances in modern science are astounding. They're almost impossible to keep up with. I subscribe to *Plastic Surgery Monthly*. I study the column called "Fab Re-Habs." You should, too.

When it comes to wrinkle removal, act now. Whether

you swing with Retin-A or the collagen thing, lose the wrinkles pronto. You'll look, feel, and sing better. If you go the plastic surgery route, be sure your doctor doesn't make your face too tight. I know a woman who had this problem. Everytime she hit a high C, it cost her $6,000.

Rugs. Ah, if only the walls would stay the same shade, the carpet would match them forever. But, people, your face isn't an apartment. As we age, our complexion loses its youthful glow and takes on a cadaverous pallor. A pretty sight? Of course not. As the skin changes color, the toupee begins to mock the face, rather than enhance it.

The time has come for a color change.

In graduating to what I call the Senior Toupee, the lounge singer is careful to select a color that complements the experienced facial tones. Oranges and maroons are wrong. Any dark color, for that matter, will create the unwanted Pudding Head Effect. Stay with the lighter hues. Soften the blow.

A note about male pattern baldness. Male pattern baldness is reassuring in the older entertainer. The classy rug knows when to retreat. Show some forehead. Dome gracefully. Avoid the Magilla Gorilla look, with the toupee an inch from your eyebrows. You'll look like you should have a banana in your hand, not a microphone.

In making yourself over, grant to age its rightful due. Allow the hands of time to caress you gently. Submit graciously to its touches—a little gray here and there, a smile line or two. In the older lounge singer, vigor must prevail. But don't overdo the youth thing—you're not in the "Little Rascals."

Where have all the globules gone,
Long time passing?
Where have all the globules gone,
Long time ago?

If I were rewriting "Where Have All the Flowers Gone?" today, I'd write it about fat. The flowers aren't going anywhere. They return with the spring.

But fat?

That's a different story. Never before in history has so much fat disappeared so quickly, and by so many exciting new methods.

It's over for fat. Vamoose. Fat's going the way of the buffalo. If you're in lard futures, get out.

This is not to say that you won't see the occasional blimp on the street. You will. And you may not enjoy it. But today, the lounge singer no longer needs to be encumbered by unsightly cellulite.

Should you wait *one second* before availing yourself of the new technology?

No.

Would Elvis have waited?

No.

The King would have had it removed by the pailful. All the old jumpsuits would have fit again. Down-sized, Elvis might be alive today.

So, music, Maestro—please. And start sucking.

Liposuction is a miracle. It's mind-boggling what modern science can do for your figure with a vacuum cleaner and a bucket. Get slim. The modern way. It'll be worth every penny.

Don't skimp on the operation. Unethical liposuction

doctors in Mexico have removed vital organs by mistake. Also, beware of any practitioner who says he can perform "psychic liposuction." This is quackery. They palm chicken fat and smear it all over you. You end up just as overweight and smelling like a Brooklyn apartment.

Do it once, and do it right. And pay top dollar as usual.

You've Been a Great Audience

Ladies and gentlemen, before I bring this book to a close, allow me to say something from the very bottom of my heart. We've written all over this nutty world. We've written high, and we've written low. We've written on mild hallucinogens and alcoholic beverages. We've written for princes, kings, queens, popes . . . saddams. But in all of our years in show business, we've never had an audience who could *read* as well as you. You are truly special. You've read every word of this, and taken each and every word to heart. As I look out at your faces, I see the promise of tomorrow.

What do you know now that you didn't know on page one? How have you been enriched? How have you learned to be more like me, Bud E. Luv?

You've learned to use the microphone. You've learned not to abuse the warm-up suit. You've learned the importance of natural fibers. You've learned the meaning of hair, the mystery of physical gestures, the power of jewelry. You've learned to believe in your talent

SUSAN MUNROE

THIS BEAUTIFUL WELSH CORGI WAS
NOT A GIFT FROM THE QUEEN, AS
REPORTED IN THE *National Enquirer*.
IT WAS A GIFT FROM ANOTHER GREAT
WELSH EXPORT—MY CLOSE PERSONAL
FRIEND TOM JONES.

and how to look talented. You've learned to enhance, maximize. You've captured the delicate butterfly of style. You've learned exquisite taste in the choice of material—in brocades as well as ballads. You've learned how to hold the little people in the palm of your hand, spellbound, and not crush them. And you've learned to pay minimum wage.

Are you a swinging cat? Yes, but you're more. You're sensitive yet strong. Single-minded yet unpredictable. You're generous to a fault, yet ever the master of your kingdom. Arabian horses, accountants, chauffeurs, broads—they're all at your beck and call. You're confident. You're regal. You're powerful. You're nauseous.

But that's because it's all *new*. Relax. Prepare to wear the mantle of greatness. The stole is laid upon your shoulders—enjoy the ermine collar. Your time has come.

I see each and every one of you—galleons on the oceans of entertainment—forging new paths through the waves, swinging in new grooves.

To me, you're more than just readers. You're a new generation of cats and kittens—a symbol of hope.

The lounge beckons. And you—armed with toupees, jewelry, medleys, moves, material, and liposuction—stand ready. You are prepared to meet the challenge. You are ready to be a lounge singer.

Who Loves Ya?

Excuse me. I'm a little choked up. I'll be all right. Thanks.

(You may wish to put on my recording of "You'll Never Walk Alone" while you're reading this.)

RETIREMENT

You see, I have a vision. A dream.

I see us standing in the wings together. Thirty seconds till you go on. I've helped you get into the tux. We've discussed your opener. A last-minute adjustment of the cuffs, a quick look in the mirror. You're ready.

I hear the band swinging into your theme song. The announcer is saying your name over the P.A. You're stepping through the curtain. You're doing the Entrance Gait. The lights are hitting you like an explosion.

The audience is going nuts.

It's your show. You're there.

You're a lounge singer.

And while you're knocking them dead with your opener, I ask just one thing—that you cast a glance to the side of the stage.

See the figure there, in the wings, with tears in his eyes.

That'll be me.

I'll always be there.

Who loves ya?

Bud E. loves ya.

Thank you. And good night.

GREAT MOMENTS

IN LOUNGE HISTORY

10,000 b.c. — First song dedication made in Lascaux caves.

1522 b.c. — Pharaoh "Tony" Ra hires first valet.

543 b.c. — Apollo bombs at Delphi.

51 b.c. — Julius Caesar gets first liquor license.

79 a.d. — First pit orchestra plays the Coliseum.

1203 — Robin Hood introduces the cape at Sherwood Forest Lounge.

1518 — Ponce de León discovers and names the Fontainebleu Lounge in Miami.

1539 — Copernicus invents the mirror ball.

1643 — Goodman Presley, inventor of the jump suit, arrives in New World.

1711 — Hans Tuchs, a Swiss, patents the tuxedo.

1743 — The ruffled shirt is introduced at Versailles.

1880 — The Liberace family enters America through Ellis Island.

1892 — Louis Chevrolet builds the first limousine; calls it a Chevrousine.

1911 — First steam-powered slot machine installed in Silver City, Colorado.

1913—Al Jolson loosens necktie during show.

1948—First toupee worn on television.

1954—First busload of gamblers arrives at Cal-Neva Lodge.

1961—First Holiday Inn Lounge opens.

B U D   E .   L U V

F A N   C L U B

For information about the Bud E. Luv Fan Club, please write to:

The Bud E. Luv Fan Club
c/o The Overland Entertainment Company
257 West Fifty-second Street
New York, N.Y. 10019